Neighborhoods, People, and Community

ENVIRONMENT, DEVELOPMENT, AND PUBLIC POLICY

A series of volumes under the general editorship of
Lawrence Susskind, *Massachusetts Institute of Technology
Cambridge, Massachusetts*

CITIES AND DEVELOPMENT

Series Editor: Lloyd Rodwin, *Massachusetts Institute of Technology
Cambridge, Massachusetts*

CITIES AND CITY PLANNING
Lloyd Rodwin

THINKING ABOUT DEVELOPMENT
Lisa Peattie

CONSERVING AMERICA'S NEIGHBORHOODS
Robert K. Yin

MAKING WORK
Self-Created Jobs in Participatory Organizations
William Ronco and Lisa Peattie

CITIES OF THE MIND
Images and Themes of the City in the Social Sciences
Lloyd Rodwin and Robert M. Hollister

NEIGHBORHOODS, PEOPLE, AND COMMUNITY
Roger S. Ahlbrandt, Jr.

Other subseries:

ENVIRONMENTAL POLICY AND PLANNING
Series Editor: Lawrence Susskind, *Massachusetts Institute of Technology,
Cambridge, Massachusetts*

PUBLIC POLICY AND SOCIAL SERVICES
Series Editor: Gary Marx, *Massachusetts Institute of Technology,
Cambridge, Massachusetts*

Neighborhoods, People, and Community

Roger S. Ahlbrandt, Jr.

University of Pittsburgh
Pittsburgh, Pennsylvania

Plenum Press · New York and London

HN
80
P6
A35
1984
c.1

Library of Congress Cataloging in Publication Data

Ahlbrandt, Roger S.
  Neighborhoods, people, and community.

  (Environment, development, and public policy. Cities and development)
  Bibliography: p.
  Includes index.
  1. Pittsburgh (Pa.)—Social conditions. 2. Neighborhood—Pennsylvania—Pittsburgh. 3. Urban policy—Pennsylvania—Pittsburgh. 4. Community life. 5. Community organization. I. Title. II. Series.
  HN80.P6A35   1984   307′.3362′0974886   84-8339
  ISBN 0-306-41542-9

©1984 Plenum Press, New York
A Division of Plenum Publishing Corporation
233 Spring Street, New York, N.Y. 10013

Printed in the United States of America

To Patty and Julie

Preface

This book focuses on neighborhoods and the people living in them. It describes differences among neighborhoods in terms of their social and institutional structure, attitudes of the residents, quality of life, and the characteristics of the residents.

The book is based on the results of a survey of almost 6,000 residents living throughout the city of Pittsburgh. As such it provides the basis for examining groups of people as well as whole neighborhoods. The communal aspects of urban living are discussed in Chapters 1 and 2; attachment toward the neighborhood in Chapter 3; importance of religion, life cycle, and race in Chapter 4; various aspects of individual social support systems and neighborhood social fabric in Chapters 5, 6, and 7; the contextual aspects of the neighborhood environment in Chapters 8 and 9; and the implications for urban policy in Chapter 10.

The results of the analysis described in the book provide a detailed understanding of differences in the structure and composition of urban neighborhoods, and they show why some groups of people are drawn into their neighborhoods whereas others rely more upon the wider community to meet a variety of needs. The analysis provides the framework in which to address the implications for urban policy, particularly with respect to mental health prevention and neighborhood and community renewal.

The analysis shows that neighborhoods are communities of limited liability. People use both the neighborhood and the wider community to meet their needs. However, for some groups of people the neighborhood is much more important than it is for others. For instance, age, income, family composition, and race make a difference. Older people, those with less income, households with children, and blacks are more dependent upon their neighborhoods than are other groups of people.

The analysis also shows that the contextual aspects of the neighborhood have an important influence on the way in which people regard their neighborhood and the uses they make of it. The neighborhood can therefore be thought of as helping to create a community of interaction among the residents—some types of neighborhoods more so than others.

The analysis provides a variety of insights for urban policymakers. The debate between place versus people as the appropriate focus for urban intervention strategies is inappropriate. Urban policy, whether it encompasses neighborhood stabilization, community development, or mental health prevention, must consider both place *and* people. People have problems which must be attended to directly, but there is a direct link between people's problems and the environment in which they live. Therefore, place must be treated as well.

For example, national housing policy could be conducted through a people-oriented strategy such as a housing voucher, or a strategy directed toward place such as new construction and rehabilitation of existing housing. Chapter 10 discusses the merits of a housing voucher, the principal one being that it increases people's options. However, reliance solely upon this approach is not appropriate for all groups of people or for all neighborhoods. The analysis in this book shows that many people are strongly attached to their neighborhood or are constrained to their neighborhood because of old age, lack of income, or race. A housing voucher will only work well for people who want to remain in their own neighborhood if there is a supply of vacant, standard quality housing. If there is not, a place-oriented strategy is still required if the needs of the people and their neighborhood are to be served. National housing policy should therefore embody both approaches because the needs of people and the availability of vacant housing will vary from one part of the country to another as well as within a particular city.

Finally, from a policy perspective, the results discussed in this book argue in favor of policies designed to strengthen the institutional structure of urban neighborhoods. This is particularly important for lower-income neighborhoods because the residents are more place-bound and have fewer options outside of their neighborhoods to meet their needs.

ROGER S. AHLBRANDT, JR.

Acknowledgments

The research discussed in this book was developed after almost 10 years of studying Pittsburgh's neighborhoods in collaboration with James V. Cunningham, Professor in the School of Social Work at the University of Pittsburgh. Jim and I have worked closely together on a number of projects and have developed a strong sense of the importance of the social aspects of the neighborhood in the lives of the residents and in determining the future of the city. I am greatly indebted to the intellectual stimulus provided by Jim as well as to his practical insights into the ways in which the social fabric of individual neighborhoods can be strengthened.

The research described in this book was made possible by a grant from the Center for Studies of Metropolitan Problems of the National Institute of Mental Health. I greatly appreciate the center's support and the guidance provided by Maury Lieberman, the project officer on the grant.

A number of people were instrumental in helping to conduct the research. The University Center for Social and Urban Research at the University of Pittsburgh conducted the fieldwork. Staff of the center worked seven days a week for 11 weeks to complete 5,896 telephone interviews, kept the project within budget, and produced a quality product. In particular, I am indebted to the following staff members of the center: Elaine McGivern for preparing the sample frame; Albert Gans for taking care of numerous details; Sadye Weiss for impeccable bookkeeping; Joyce Slater for supervising the coding of the questionnaire; Stephanie

Gonos for keypunching the data; Laurie Fowler for programming assistance and for helping to proofread and edit the final manuscript; and Chris Bottles and Mildred Asbury for typing several parts of the final manuscript.

Special thanks go to Steve Manners, who was responsible for supervising all of the programming in connection with the data analysis phase of the project. Through his efforts a mountain of computer output was obtained. In addition, a debt of eternal gratitude is owed to Marty Denoff and Jennifer Newman. They supervised the entire field operation and had the extremely difficult task of motivating the interviewers and at the same time producing a quality product within a very tight time schedule. They did an outstanding job and convinced me that the success of a field research project is decided in large part by the quality of the field supervisors. Also 42 people participated at some point as interviewers and I am greatly indebted to them.

I wish to thank David Epperson, Dean of the School of Social Work, for his encouragement and support throughout the project. Linda Wykoff typed numerous drafts, and I am grateful for her careful scrutiny of the manuscript. I also wish to thank the large number of people who have contributed to my thinking over the years and who have in an indirect way influenced the direction of my research. Finally, Gerald Suttles reviewed previous drafts of this manuscript and made numerous helpful suggestions.

Contents

List of Tables

CHAPTER 1

A Community Focus

INTRODUCTION

This book is about people, their neighborhoods, and their relevant community of action. The research findings discussed in the following pages are organized to provide a greater understanding of the concept of community in the lives of urban residents today. The spatial distribution of the social relationships that people have with one another is analyzed, and the concept of neighborhood is then examined in terms of what forms of involvement, commitment, and investment individuals undertake in that area.

The focus of the book is on the internal structure of urban neighborhoods and the factors associated with the composition and extensiveness of the social relationships of the residents. These relationships include primary ties, such as family, friends, and providers of emotional supports; secondary relationships, such as the neighboring that occurs; and membership in voluntary organizations.

By focusing upon the relationships that people have with one another and the location of the various activities in which people are engaged, the relevant community of action for neighborhood residents is constructed. The findings show that the concept of community varies for different groups of people and that the community of action for most people extends beyond the boundaries of their neighborhood. This does not imply that the neighborhood is not a focal point for communal activities. It is most important for those who are restricted to place for a variety of reasons, but it is also used—albeit somewhat differently—by those who have the greatest choice of where to socialize and participate.

People's concepts of community as applied to their neighborhood vary depending upon the types of relationships the individuals maintain and the types of activities they pursue in the neighborhood. Those in turn are influenced by the opportunities that people have for participation outside the neighborhood and by the relative attractiveness of the neighborhood in terms of the quality of the environment and the opportunities for social and institutional interaction. This means that the strength of communal bonds within a neighborhood is dependent upon a number of factors which include the characteristics of the population and the characteristics of the neighborhood. The research findings reported in this book give insights into these relationships. They also provide a necessary starting point for a better understanding of urban neighborhoods, which are the building blocks of cities.

CONCEPT OF COMMUNITY

The concept of the community[1] of limited liability or one of the other conceptualizations of a community that extends outward from an individual's immediate surroundings stands juxtaposed against the idea of the traditional local community. The latter emphasizes the involuntary or coercive aspects of locality: the way local communities once confined their residents because of limited mobility, parochialism, and ascriptive social relations. The former brings into relief the more voluntaristic character of local

---

[1]The author wishes to thank Gerald D. Suttles for his comments on this section.

communities in modern industrial society. In these circumstances, participation in the local community is more voluntaristic, something that people choose to undertake, something they may undertake only as the circumstance arises, or something that they may neglect to do altogether.[2]

The community of limited liability was conceived of as an alternative to widespread forecasts of the decline of community, an argument that the local community would simply disappear as the traditional community lost its hold. Repeated findings show that this simply does not happen. Rather, given the choice, some people continue to participate in the local community, to give it their time, their loyalty, their energy. They do so conditionally rather than unconditionally—hence the concept of limited liability. Communities, like other organizations, must attract participants by positive rewards and gratifications, and when they fail to do so people will withdraw their commitment, participation, and investments. In any event, their commitments are seldom so irrevocable as in the traditional community.

Of course, the traditional community has not entirely disappeared. Individual characteristics and social circumstances may still restrict some people almost wholly to the

[2]For example, see Scott Greer, *The Emerging City* (New York: Free Press, 1962); Albert Hunter, *Symbolic Communities* (Chicago: University of Chicago Press, 1974); Morris Janowitz, *The Community Press in an Urban Setting* (Chicago: University of Chicago Press, 1967); Gerald D. Suttles, *The Social Construction of Communities* (Chicago: University of Chicago Press, 1972); Duncan W. G. Timms, *The Urban Mosaic: Towards a Theory of Residential Differentiation* (Cambridge, England: Cambridge University Press, 1971): pp. 329–50; Rachelle B. Warren and Donald I. Warren, *The Neighborhood Organizer's Handbook* (Notre Dame, Ind.: The University of Notre Dame Press, 1977); Melvin M. Webber, "Order in Diversity: Community Without Propinquity," in *Neighborhood, City and Metropolis,* eds. Robert Gutman and David Popenoe (New York: Random House, 1970); and Barry Wellman, "The Intimate Networks of East Yonkers," *American Journal of Sociology* 84 (March 1979): 1201–31.

local community. For children and the aged, the local community may constitute almost the entirety of their face-to-face world. Both the community of limited liability and the traditional community are ideal types; neither is fully realized in actual life. Thus, in contemporary American life one can conceive of a general dimension spanning the difference between individuals who have a very wide range of choices including participation in the local community and others whose range of choices is so restricted that it includes only the local community and, sometimes, not even that.

The study discussed in this book explores the conditions under which people involve themselves in their local community. To a very large extent, the findings show that the local community is a voluntary construction. People are drawn to the community by its attractions—quality of life, social fabric, institutions, and personal ties to the other residents—so that communities differ considerably in their ability to incorporate the loyalties and energies of their members. Of course, there are individuals, especially the aged, those with less income, and sometimes blacks, whose involvement seems less voluntary and less satisfying. People of different background also differ considerably in their ability to construct local communities that are rewarding. Catholics seem especially able to do so; blacks, far less so. There are differences as well in the orientation of some subgroups apparently leading them to look for and find communities that permit higher or more satisfying involvement. To a considerable extent it is by finding one another that these people create such satisfactory communities. All of this leads to the conclusion that the availability of choice in modern industrial societies is not antithetical to the local community; certainly a greater choice promotes wider associational ties beyond the local community, but it does not keep people from being involved and participating in the local community. People seem simply to have a wider range of associational life, and it continues to include the local community.

THE RESEARCH CONTEXT

This research was conducted in the city of Pittsburgh during 1980. Like many older cities in the northeastern and central United States, Pittsburgh has experienced a net outmigration of its population during the past 20 years. During the period from 1960 to 1980, the city's population fell from 604,000 to 424,000, with a net loss of about 97,000 people during the 1970s. Pittsburgh is located in Allegheny County, and similar trends were observed there. Allegheny County's population declined slightly during the 1960s, from 1,628,000 to 1,605,000 people, but then fell by 155,000 during the 1970s to its current level of 1,450,000 residents.

The large population decline in the city has not undermined the housing market of individual neighborhoods to the extent one might expect, and there are no large pockets of abandonment in the city. The effects of the population loss in the city have been muted by (1) a decrease in the household size, which has resulted in a less-than-proportional reduction in the demand for housing, (2) the city's urban renewal and spot demolition programs, which have removed abandoned units on a regular basis, and (3) the fact that the population decline has not been concentrated in a few neighborhoods but instead has been spread over most parts of the city. At least on the surface, most of Pittsburgh's neighborhoods appear to be strong, healthy communities.

Pittsburgh is an ideal city in which to conduct a study of urban neighborhoods because the boundaries of its neighborhoods are well defined and have changed relatively little over time. In 1975, the author participated in a neighborhood boundary identification project, the Pittsburgh Neighborhood Atlas,[3] which held forty workshops

---

[3]Roger S. Ahlbrandt, Jr., Margaret Charny, and James V. Cunningham, "Citizen Perceptions of Their Neighborhoods," *Journal of Housing* 34 (July 1977): 338–41.

throughout the city for residents to map the boundaries of their neighborhoods. Seventy-eight distinct neighborhoods, comprising all parts of the city, were identified in the workshops.

The boundaries of the neighborhoods used in this book are based to a great extent on those developed in the Pittsburgh Neighborhood Atlas project. However, several large neighborhoods were subdivided, a few small neighborhoods were combined, and whole census tracts were used for purposes of aggregation (a few neighborhoods in the Atlas project split census tracts—the split tracts were combined and placed in a single neighborhood because some of the data gathered in this research were only available on a whole census tract basis). For the purposes of this project, Pittsburgh was divided into 74 separate neighborhoods, ranging in size from 900 to 25,000 residents. The average neighborhood contains approximately 2,500 households.

Those interviewed for this study were aware of the neighborhood in which they lived. Ninety-three percent identified their neighborhood by name, and 68% said that it had definite boundaries.

THE SURVEY

Data for the study were collected through a telephone survey of a random sample of Pittsburgh residents. The sample, drawn from Cole's Directory, was stratified by neighborhood on the basis of its proportion of city households. Within each neighborhood an interval sample of listed telephone subscribers was drawn to ensure proportionate representation of each block within the neighborhood. The head-of-household or spouse (18 years of age or older) was interviewed. Thirteen percent of the telephone numbers were found to be disconnected. Of those remaining, a 42% response rate was achieved. Approximately 3% of the households in each neighborhood were interviewed.

The primary disadvantage of the telephone survey

technique is that people who do not have telephone numbers or whose numbers are unlisted are excluded from the sample. To the extent the characteristics of this group differ significantly from those having a listed telephone number, a bias will be built into the results. There was no *a priori* reason to believe that this would be a problem for this project[4] because the number of households without a phone is small. At worst, the results would not be generalizable to that population.

The advantages of the telephone survey for a project of this magnitude far outweigh any potential disadvantages. The benefits include:

- *Lower cost.* The cost of the telephone survey was approximately 30% of what it would have cost to conduct personal interviews. This is a result of a more efficient interviewing process—there is no travel time and call backs are easily arranged (7% of the completed interviews were conducted at a time more convenient to the respondent than that of the original phone contact).
- *Better quality control.* The interviewers worked in the same office, two or three interviewers to a room. A field supervisor was always present. This provided a number of advantages. Questions of individual interviewers were answered immediately; this was particularly important in the early phase of the project. Completed questionnaires were reviewed immediately for new interviewers and always by the next day. If they were improperly filled out, the interviewer was shown the proper procedure and the respondent was called back if necessary. Finally, the presence of a supervisor and other interviewers in the room minimized the temptation to "fake" an

---

[4] For a discussion of a comparison of telephone and personal interviews see Robert M. Groves and Robert L. Kahn, *Surveys by Telephone: A National Comparison with Personal Interviews* (New York: Academic Press, 1979).

interview. (The supervisor called back one out of every 10 respondents to check on the accuracy of the interview.)

- *Fewer weeks in the field.* The 5,896 interviews were completed in 11 weeks (the average interview required approximately 25 minutes). It is unlikely that personal interviews could have been completed in as short a period of time unless the number of interviewers was substantially increased. As it was, 42 interviewers worked on the project, approximately 20 at any one time. A significantly larger group would have been unmanageable, and quality would have suffered. Also, since the number of completed questionnaires per interviewer was monitored daily, the performance of each interviewer could be followed and extra assistance provided to those who were consistently slow.
- *A more representative sample.* In order to ensure that working and nonworking households were proportionately represented in the sample, the interviews were conducted Monday through Friday from 4:00 P.M. to 9:00 P.M., and on Saturday and Sunday from 1:00 P.M. to 5:00 P.M. Had the interviews been conducted during the normal working day, the working head-of-household would have been underrepresented. Personal interviews would not have worked well during the hours chosen for this project because the fieldwork occurred between January and March. It is normally dark in the late afternoon, and it would have been very difficult to get interviewers to work in unfamiliar parts of the city at night.
- *High motivation.* Because the interviewers worked in an office setting and could interact with each other and their supervisor, greater comradery developed than would have occurred in the case of a personal interview project. This esprit de corps raised the commitment of the interviewers to the project and undoubtedly increased the quality of the interviews and reduced turnover.

The characteristics of the telephone interview sample were not significantly different from the population as a whole except for homeownership. Median household income for the sample was $13,200 compared to $13,400 reported by the United States Census for the city of Pittsburgh. (The census data were collected at about the same time the survey was being conducted.) The 22% black population in the sample compares favorably to the 24% reported by the census, but the homeownership rate of 63% is much higher than the census figure of 51%. This is as expected. The proportionate representation of the sample by neighborhood would be expected to produce comparable income and racial characteristics. The higher homeownership rate is accounted for by the fact that homeowners are more likely to have a phone than renters.

Survey questions were asked on the following subject areas: sense of community, local facility use, neighborhood conditions, satisfaction with public services, willingness to remain in the neighborhood, neighboring activities, social support systems, participation in voluntary organizations, work, housing, health, life satisfaction, happiness, and socioeconomic characteristics. (Appendix C at the conclusion of the book contains the survey instrument used to collect the data.) Other data were gathered from a survey of neighborhood organizations in the city of Pittsburgh.

WHAT FOLLOWS

The research findings are discussed in the following sections. Chapter 2 examines the survey data on an individual basis and presents evidence in support of the community of limited liability; variations in the extent of internal and external neighborhood ties are shown to be a function of the choices and constraints confronting the residents. Chapter 3 discusses the factors associated with affective sentiments and shows that various aspects of the neighborhood as well as the characteristics of the residents play an important role in creating community; the feeling of neighborhood attachment is shown to be influenced to a much greater extent by the social fabric of the neighborhood, whereas the respondent's satisfaction with the neighborhood as a place to live is more dependent upon the amenities that the neighborhood has to offer. Chapter 4 shows that differences in religion, life cycle, and race explain variations in the reasons that people give for moving into the neighborhood, their attachment to it, what they like or dislike about it, and the extensiveness of their neighborhood personal network. Chapter 5 examines the relationship between various elements of the neighborhood's social support system and people's reported health, happiness, and life satisfaction; the analysis shows that the neighborhood's personal support structure and its institutional base are positively related to happiness and life satisfaction.

After Chapter 5, the book turns from an analysis at the individual level to one that focuses upon the neighborhood and variation across neighborhoods. Chapter 6 analyzes the concept of social fabric in detail, showing that the elements that comprise the social fabric of the neighborhood are distinct and may vary independently of one another. Chapter 7 investigates the relationship between the social fabric of the neighborhood and neighborhood change defined in economic terms. (This link is observed only in the short run; over the longer term the institutional base of the neighborhood is of more importance.) Chapter 8 studies the contextual influence of the neighborhood by categorizing neighborhoods on the basis of their racial composition and by comparing differences in attitudes, social fabric, and other variables across the neighborhood groups for respondents of similar race and income; the analysis shows that contextual effects are present and that they influence the communal bonds within the neighborhoods. Chapter 9 classifies neighborhoods on the basis of mean household income and analyzes differences among the groups as well as within each group; the latter approach highlights the importance of analyzing neighborhoods on an individual basis and illustrates the significance of ethnicity in determining the strength of the social fabric in many of the moderate-income neighborhoods. The chapter also demonstrates that community can be constructed by a number of the variables that form the contextual environment of the neighborhood. Finally, Chapter 10 contains a discussion of the policy implications of the research.

CHAPTER 2

The Community of Action

INTRODUCTION

Recent community-related research presents a growing body of evidence in support of the notion of a community without propinquity, a community of limited liability or a liberated community. Studies have shown that urbanites not only are involved in their own solidarity but are likely to be linked to others as well. The evidence documents the persistence of primary ties which are not restricted to a densely knit solidarity but form a spatially diverse network which transcends kin and neighborhood to encompass a wide range of relationships throughout the city and beyond.[1]

---

[1]See D. Cooperman and L. Hagoel, "Community in Southdale," *CURA Reporter* 10 (June 1980): 12–15; Claude S. Fischer, Robert M. Jackson, C. Ann Stueve, Kathleen Gerson, and Lynne McCallister-Jones, with Mark Baldassare, *Networks and Places* (New York: Free Press, 1977); Mark Granovetter, "The Strength of Weak Ties," *American Journal of Sociology* 78 (May 1973): 1360–80; Scott Greer, *The Emerging City* (New York: Free Press, 1962); Albert Hunter, *Symbolic Communities* (Chicago: University of Chicago Press, 1974); Morris Janowitz, *The Community Press in an Urban Setting* (Chicago: University of Chicago Press, 1967); Edward O. Laumann, *Bonds of Pluralism* (New York: Wiley, 1973); Gerald D. Suttles, *The Social Construction of Communities* (Chicago: University of Chicago Press, 1972); Duncan W. G. Timms, *The Urban Mosaic: Towards a Theory of Residential Differentiation* (Cambridge, England: Cambridge University Press, 1971); Gerald Walker, "Social Networks and Territory

Research by Laumann, Fischer, Warren, Wellman, and others has used a social network perspective to identify the relevant community for a particular person or group of individuals.[2] A network approach makes no *a priori* assumption about community boundaries. Through interviews, individuals are asked to identify their friends and/ or people upon whom they rely for assistance in time of need. By identifying the most important actors in an individual's network and by locating where these people live, networking permits the researcher to construct the community of action for those being studied.[3]

Analyzing community by studying an individual's primary ties frees community theorists from the limitation of a strict territorial perspective. The territorial approach, by implicitly assuming a predefined set of boundaries for community, usually a neighborhood, constrains the analysis of kinship ties, organizational activities, and shared senti-

---

in A Commuter Village, Bond Head, Ontario," *Canadian Geographer* 21 (Winter 1977): 329–50; Donald I. Warren, *Helping Networks: How People Cope with Problems in the Urban Community* (Notre Dame, Ind: The University of Notre Dame Press, 1981); Rachelle B. Warren and Donald I. Warren, *The Neighborhood Organizer's Handbook* (Notre Dame, Ind: The University of Notre Dame Press, 1977); Melvin M. Webber, "Order in Diversity: Community Without Propinquity," in *Neighborhood, City and Metropolis,* ed. Robert Gutman and David Popenoe (New York: Random House, 1970); and Barry Wellman, "The Community Question: The Intimate Networks of East Yonkers," *American Journal of Sociology* 84 (March 1979): 1201–31.

[2]See Laumann, *Bonds of Pluralism;* Fischer *et al., Networks and Places;* Warren, *Helping Networks;* Wellman, "The Community Question: The Intimate Networks of East Yonkers."

[3]For a discussion of the network perspective, see Richard Emerson, "Power–Dependence Relations," *American Sociological Review* 27 (February 1962): 31–41; J. Clyde Mitchell, "The Concept and Use of Social Networks," in *Social Networks in Urban Situations,* ed. J. Clyde Mitchell (Manchester: University of Manchester Press, 1969); James Allen Barnes, *Social Networks* (Reading, Ma.: Addison-Wesley, 1972); Paul Craven and Barry Wellman, "The Network City," *Sociological Inquiry* 43 (1973): 58–88; Fischer *et al., Networks and Places;* and Barry Wellman and Barry Leighton, "Networks, Neighborhoods and Communities: Approaches to the Study of the Community Question," *Urban Affairs Quarterly* 14 (March 1979): 363–90.

ments to that particular area. This approach implicitly assumes that communal ties can only be found in corporate groups, such as neighborhoods, which provide the context for multiple ties and frequent interaction. If these ties are found to be weak, theorists argue that community is "lost";[4] if the ties remain strong, arguments are made that community is "saved."[5]

A territorial perspective provides insight into the extent to which community is present within a bounded geographic area, but if the analysis is limited only to what occurs within the prescribed boundaries, it obscures the links that exist outside of the area. A network analysis identifies these relationships, but unless the research also focuses upon the local area in which people live, the role of place in the urban area is obscured.[6]

The literature has shown that people are attached to their place of residence in a variety of ways;[7] still, as net-

[4]See Maurice R. Stein, *The Eclipse of Community* (New York: Harper & Row, 1960); Robert A. Nisbet, *The Quest for Community* (New York: Oxford University Press, 1969); and Joe Feagin, "Community Disorganization," *Sociological Inquiry* 43 (Winter 1973): 123–46.

[5]William Foote Whyte, *Street Corner Society*, Enlarged Edition (Chicago: University of Chicago Press, 1955); Herbert J. Gans, *The Urban Villagers* (New York: Free Press, 1962); Herbert J. Gans, *The Levittowners* (New York: Vintage, 1967); Elliott Liebow, *Tally's Corner* (Boston: Little Brown, 1967); Gerald D. Suttles, *The Social Order of the Slum* (Chicago: University of Chicago Press, 1968): and Carol B. Stack, *All Our Kin* (New York: Harper & Row, 1974).

[6]This point is well developed by Wellman and Leighton, "Networks, Neighborhoods and Communities: Approaches to the Study of the Community Question." A good analysis of the role of place in 16 black and 12 white neighborhoods is contained in Donald I. Warren, "Explorations in Neighborhood Differentiation," *Sociological Quarterly* 19 (Spring 1973): 310–31.

[7]John D. Kasarda and Morris Janowitz, "Community Attachment in Mass Society," *American Sociological Review* 39 (June 1974): 328–39; Albert Hunter, "The Loss of Community," *American Sociological Review* 40 (October 1975): 537–552; William Michelson, *Environmental Choice, Human Behavior and Residential Satisfaction* (New York: Oxford University Press, 1977); and Roger S. Ahlbrandt, Jr., and James V. Cunningham, *A New Public Policy for Neighborhood Preservation* (New York: Praeger, 1979), Ch. 5.

work theorists have shown, people are engaged in meaningful relationships outside of their immediate residential
environment. The concept of community therefore consists
of a number of different dimensions. There is the locality
or place that serves certain functions and there is the
extralocal community into which people's networks also
extend. Both concepts of community are important to a person's social and psychological well-being. Each provides
certain types of services and supports which help people
function and lessen their alienation.[8] Therefore, investi-

[8]For examples of literature which discuss the relationship between com-
munity resources, informal social support systems and mental health, see
Phyllis Silverman, "The Widow to Widow Program: An Experiment in
Preventive Intervention," *Mental Hygiene* 53 (1969): 333–37; Elizabeth
Bott, *Family and Social Network: Norms and External Relationships in
Ordinary Urban Families* (London: Tavistock 2nd ed. rev., 1971); Eugene
Litwak and Ivan Szelenyi, "Primary Group Structures and Their Func-
tions: Kin, Neighbors and Friends," *American Sociological Review* 34
(August 1969): 465–81; Barry Wellman, Paul Craven, Marilyn Whitaker,
Sheila Dutoit, and Harvey Stevens, "The Uses of Community," Research
Paper No. 47 (Center for Urban and Community Studies, University of
Toronto, 1971); Gerald Caplan, *Support Systems and Community Mental
Health: Lectures on Concept Development* (New York: Behavioral Publi-
cations, 1974); Carolyn L. Attneave, "Social Networks as the Unit of
Intervention," in *Family Therapy: Theory and Practice,* ed. P. J. Guerin,
pp. 220–32 (New York: Gardner Press, 1976); Gerald Caplan and Marie
Killilea, *Support Systems and Mutual Help* (New York: Grune & Stratton,
1976); Alice Collins and Diane Pancoast, *Natural Helping Networks*
(Washington, D.C.: National Association of Social Workers, 1976); Ber-
tram H. Kaplan, John C. Cassel, and Susan Gore, "Social Support and
Health," *Medical Care* 15 (1977): 47–58 (supplement); Susan Gore,
"The Effects of Social Support in Moderating the Health Consequences of
Unemployment," *Journal of Health and Social Behavior* 19 (1978): 157–
65; Nan Lin, Walter Ensel, Ronald Simeone, and Wen Kuo, "Social Sup-
port, Stressful Life Events and Illness: A Model and an Empirical Test,"
Journal of Health and Social Behavior 29 (1979): 108–19; James House,
Work Stress and Mental Health (Reading, MA: Addison-Wesley, 1980);
and David Biegel and Arthur Naparstek, eds., *Community Support Systems and Mental Health* (New York: Springer, 1982). A review of the literature is contained in President's Commission on Mental Health, *Task
Panel Reports Submitted to the President's Commission on Mental
Health, Vol. II* (Washington, D.C.: U. S. Government Printing Office,
1978).

gations into community must examine the ways in which people are attached to their locality as well as focusing on their commitments outside of that area.

This chapter investigates the concept of community from both a territorial and network perspective. The territorial approach uses neighborhoods as the relevant locality and analyzes attachment to place in terms of institutional ties, neighboring, organizational involvement, neighborhood friends, and kin. People's social networks are examined in terms of intimate ties. The most important individuals in the network are identified and compared according to the content of the relationship and place of residence.

The framework for the analysis is drawn from a choice-constraint model of human behavior. This assumes that people operate in their own best interests given the opportunities available to them, the constraints upon their behavior, and their tastes, preferences, and values.[9] The model hypothesizes that people's behavior will be influenced by a number of factors, such as age, income, life cycle, family composition, race, and ethnicity, and that therefore differences among groups must be taken into account. The research reported upon in this chapter examines group differences in terms of income, age, family composition, and race.

Age is viewed as a constraint to behavior because as people grow older their diminished mobility reduces their ability to maintain ties outside of their neighborhood. Therefore, elderly people should be more dependent upon their place of residence for the services it provides, and likewise, their social network may be more restricted geographically.

---

[9]For a discussion of a constraint maximizing model of human behavior, see Georg Simmel, *Conflict and the Web of Group Affiliations*, trans. by K. H. Wolff and R. H. Bendix (New York: Free Press, 1922, 1955); J. Thibaut and H. H. Kelly, *The Social Psychology of Groups* (New York: Wiley, 1959); George C. Homans, *Social Behavior*, 2nd ed. (New York: Harcourt Brace Jovanovich, 1974); and Claude S. Fischer *et al., Networks and Places.*

Income constrains behavior because it limits people's opportunities. It is costly to engage in many activities outside of the neighborhood and to maintain social and emotional ties over longer distances; therefore, it is reasonable to expect that higher-income households would be more likely to undertake activities or maintain relationships at greater distances from their home than lower-income persons.

Family composition may constrain behavior because households with children will be less mobile than those without. Children, particularly younger children, will have playmates in the neighborhood, will stay close to home, and will probably attend school in or near the neighborhood. These activities will bring the parents into close contact with others in the neighborhood and should increase the opportunity for interaction. Households with children, headed by a single parent, may be more constrained to place because of a lower income than that of a two-parent family, and widowed households may be more place-bound because of the age factor.

Racial differences may be associated with variations in attachment or social networks because race is so closely related to other characteristics of the population. In this study, the median household income of black respondents was 38% less than that of white respondents and therefore race, in part, captures the behavioral effects associated with lower income. In addition, black respondents may be more constrained to place because of past (and present) housing-market discrimination, and they will probably have fewer choices of location. If they are restricted to place not because of choice but because of few housing alternatives, their attitudes about place may be more negative than those of comparable white households.

DISCUSSION OF THE RESEARCH FINDINGS

The research findings provide ample evidence in support of the community of limited liability. The community of action for many individuals includes their neighborhood but extends beyond the neighborhood as well.

Personal Network

Interpersonal relationships within the neighborhood are extensive for many people. The percentage of respondents with kin in the neighborhood is high (44%); almost all respondents report having friends in the neighborhood (75% have at least one); and a majority (55%) of those interviewed have their primary social contact living in their neighborhood (Table 1). However, people's most intimate ties, the person or persons upon whom they rely for emotional supports, do not live in the neighborhood for approximately 70% of those interviewed, and almost half of the respondents turned to people other than kin (Table 2).

Approaching the concept of community from a network perspective, therefore, shows that the most important people in an individual's network are not restricted to kin

Table 1. Person with Whom Respondent Visits Most Often[a]

Question	Percentage of total respondents
Relationship to respondent	
Relative	12
Co-worker	9
Member of church	7
Member of other organization	2
Other	70
	100
Place of residence	
Neighborhood	55
City	31
Suburbs	12
Other	2
	100

[a]Based on survey of neighborhood residents in city of Pittsburgh (N = 5,896).

Table 2. Persons on Whom Respondent Relies for Emotional Support[a]

Question	Percentage of total respondents	
	Person 1	Person 2
Relationship to respondent		
Parent	10	8
Brother/sister	18	16
Child	13	14
Relative	11	12
Co-worker	5	5
Neighbor	5	5
Minister	2	1
Other	4	4
Friend	32	35
	100	100
Place of residence		
Neighborhood	32	28
City	41	39
Suburbs	17	19
Pennsylvania	4	5
Outside of Pennsylvania	6	9
	100	100

[a]Based on survey of neighborhood residents in city of Pittsburgh ($N = 5,896$).

and live in a variety of places throughout the city and beyond, including the neighborhood. However, while supporting an extended or liberated community, the research results also underscore the importance of place.

Role of Place

The local community or neighborhood is shown to serve a number of functions for those who live there. In addition to being the place of residence of the primary provider of emotional and social support for many people, the neighborhood provides its residents a variety of services— almost half of the respondents use facilities for shopping and/or religious, health, and recreational services in or near their place of residence (Table 3). Neighboring activities are important for almost half of those interviewed and almost all respondents believe they could turn to neighbors if an emergency arose (Table 4). In addition, organizational involvement within the neighborhood is high (17% belong to a neighborhood organization and 35% participate in other organizations in or near the neighborhood). Also, the neighborhood is an important workplace for certain groups of people. Twenty percent of those who are or were attached to the labor force work in or near the neighborhood, and the percentage is considerably higher for part-time workers.

Socioeconomic Constraints

The findings also show that place and community play different roles in the lives of different groups of individuals. (The detailed analysis upon which this discussion is based is contained in Appendix A at the end of this chapter.) Older respondents had more good friends living in the neighborhood, were more likely to rely upon neighborhood residents for emotional and social supports, and were less likely to turn to their kin than were younger individuals.

Table 3. Utilization of Neighborhood Facilities[a]

Question	Percentage of total respondents
How often do you _____ in or near your neighborhood?	Most or all of the time[b]
Shop for groceries	63
Shop for small items	45
Attend religious services	51
Use health services	45
Use recreation facilities	20

[a]Based on survey of neighborhood residents in city of Pittsburgh ($N = 5,896$).
[b]Response categories were: none, some, most or all of the time; preceding each of these questions was one which asked whether or not the service or facility was available in the neighborhood; the respondents answering that question no were coded as none in the above questions.

Table 4. Interaction with Neighbors[a]

Question[b]	Percentage of total respondents
1. If an emergency arose in your home such as an accident requiring the assistance of adults, could you call on your neighbors for help? Percentage yes	93
2. Within the past year, how often have people in this neighborhood helped you or have you helped them with small tasks such as repair work or grocery shopping? Percentage sometimes or often	60
3. How often do you visit with your neighbors? Percentage sometimes or often	50
4. How often do you borrow from or exchange things with your neighbors? Percentage sometimes or often	26

[a]Based on survey of neighborhood residents in city of Pittsburgh ($N = 5,896$).
[b]Response categories were yes or no for Question 1 and never, rarely, sometimes, or often for Questions 2–4.

The latter point may be explained by the facts that the elderly have fewer relatives currently alive or that these individuals live at distances too great to maintain active relationships. On the other hand, older respondents even in their own neighborhood are more isolated. They are less likely to neighbor or to use neighborhood-based facilities, and they turn to others for emotional support at lower rates than the rest of the population. The data underscore the importance of age as a constraint upon people's behavior. As people age, they become more restricted geographically and place becomes more important, and even within their neighborhood the elderly become more place-bound.

Income was also shown to constrain behavior. Compared to lower income respondents, those with higher incomes were more likely to socialize with people living outside of the neighborhood and to rely for emotional supports on those living beyond the boundaries of their place of residence. Higher-income respondents were also more likely to participate in voluntary organizations and to use neighborhood facilities. As incomes increased, those interviewed neighbored more and were increasingly willing to talk over their personal problems with other people. Therefore, lower-income respondents were more isolated in the sense of not only being constrained geographically but also by being less willing to interact with their neighbors.

Racial differences provide an important explanation of the variations found in many of the variables examined. Compared to black respondents, whites were more likely to go outside of the neighborhood for social and emotional supports. Whites were also more likely to talk over their personal problems and to engage in neighboring activities than were black respondents. Blacks were therefore more isolated than whites. This may be explained, in part, by the lower income of the black respondents, which makes it financially burdensome to maintain contacts at longer distances; but it may also reflect differences in either the need of blacks to engage in interpersonal contact or in the neighborhood conditions in black residential areas which make these contacts less appealing. There is some evidence to suggest that the latter is the case. Blacks go outside of their neighborhood for shopping, church, and recreation to a greater extent than whites. These facilities are not only less likely to be available in the neighborhoods inhabited by blacks, but even when they are available, black respondents use them less frequently. This could reflect a poorer quality of services or services which at least do not meet the needs of the black residents. Either of these conditions would lead to lower levels of satisfaction on the part of the black respondents. (Seventy-one percent of the white respondents were satisfied with the way the city provided services in their neighborhood compared to 54% of the blacks.)

Differences in the characteristics of the head-of-household and in the composition of the household also explain variations in the behavioral and attitudinal questions. As hypothesized, households with children are more involved in the neighborhood. They neighbor more frequently and they are involved in neighborhood-based organizations to a greater extent. However, households with children have fewer good friends in the neighborhood than do those without. This may be explained by the fact that caring for children reduces the time that the head-of-household has to develop relationships outside of the household and therefore respondents with children focus on a few important relationships rather than trying to maintain a larger number of more superficial ones. Widowed and separated and divorced households with children are the most likely to have the people they rely on for emotional supports living in the neighborhood, whereas single and separated and divorced households without children are the least likely to have these supports nearby. Most of the differences among household types can be explained in terms of age or the presence or absence of children.

The findings show that the individual characteristics of the residents are important explanatory variables for the types of uses made of the neighborhood and for differences in the composition of the social and emotional support networks. A young, single, upper-income person will behave very differently from an older, married, lower-income couple, and consequently the conclusions about neighborhood and community will vary depending upon the group being studied. As a result, the characteristics of a given population must be taken into account in the analysis of place and community.

DISCUSSION

A number of relationships have been discussed in the previous pages. In order to examine some of them in a more systematic manner, we have devised a typology which traces variations in the characteristics of residents as their primary community of action expanded. The analysis shows that only about 1% of the households were relatively isolated—neither having close personal relationships nor participating in neighborhood or voluntary organizations of any type—whereas half of those interviewed participated in and/or maintained close personal relationships both within and outside of the neighborhood (see Table 5).

Table 5. *Selected Characteristics of the Respondents by Their Primary Locus of Involvement*

Neighborhood or community involvement[a]	Median household income (in dollars)	Percentage of homeownership	Percentage black	Percentage Catholic	Number in household	Number of children less than 18 years of age	Average age of respondents	Mean years lived in neighborhood	Percentage married (single)	Number of respondents
1. Little or none	7,240	49	29	34	2.3	.5	58	22	49 (17)	69
2. Primarily within the neighborhood	11,425	66	22	53	3.0	.8	51	26	54 (18)	1,568
3. Primarily outside of the neighborhood	13,600	55	20	45	2.5	.7	45	17	48 (28)	1,405
4. Both within and outside of the neighborhood	13,675	65	22	45	2.8	.9	48	21	56 (20)	2,807

[a]The groups were constructed by placing respondents in one of the four categories based upon their answers to survey questions concerned with (a) involvement in a neighborhood organization, (b) involvement in other voluntary organizations and the location thereof, (c) place of residence of best social friend, and (d) place of residence of the primary provider of emotional supports. Respondents who did not belong to any voluntary organization and did not report having a best social friend or a provider or emotional supports were put in Group 1. Respondents whose organizational involvement and/or primary ties were only within the neighborhood were placed in Group 2. Those whose organizational involvement and/or primary ties were only outside of the neighborhood were put in Group 3. Those belonging to organizations and/or having primary ties both inside and outside of the neighborhood were put in Group 4.

The typology underscores the relevance of the choice-constraint framework. The individuals who are the most isolated have the greatest constraints on their ability to interact—they are poorer and older than the others. Those who involve themselves in the wider community face the fewest constraints on their mobility—they are younger and have higher incomes.

People who are involved in the neighborhood, regardless of whether or not they participate outside of the neighborhood, were more likely to be married, have children and own a home, factors which provide an incentive for engaging in activities closer to their home. Those who participate only in the wider community are slightly less likely to have these characteristics. In addition, individuals participating only in the wider community are younger and have lived in the neighborhood a shorter period of time than the others. People participating only in the neighborhood are the most likely to be Catholic, a tribute to the strong drawing power of neighborhood Catholic churches.

This typology emphasizes the role played by the socio-economic characteristics of the residents in determining their community of action. People are pulled inward if their other alternatives are limited by lack of income, old age, or the presence of children in the household. Home owner-ship, because it increases a person's financial stake, also provides an incentive for greater participation in the neighborhood. The neighborhood also can draw people inward because of certain amenities it offers, such as the presence of a religious institution.

Therefore, the community of action for an individual may be influenced not only by that person's position in the economic and life cycle spectrum, but also by the relative attractiveness of the possible communities in which that person could participate. A neighborhood, if it offers the type of people an individual is likely to seek out, or if it provides the types of recreational or organizational activities that appeal to the individual, will stimulate involvement, and by doing so it will help create local community attachments.

This chapter has shown that people participate to varying degrees in a number of different locations. The community of action is influenced by people's economic positions and stages in life cycle and also by the type of activity in question. The neighborhood is the relevant focal point for many people, but even those who participate in it to the greatest extent maintain intimate social networks outside of their neighborhoods.

Although the research does not offer positive proof that communities can be created, it is very suggestive. People are shown to use the neighborhood for a variety of activities and to meet a number of needs. Given the choices facing individuals, it only stands to reason that they will be inclined to gravitate toward those people and those places that can best satisfy their desires within the constraints that they face. The relative attractiveness of alternative communities of action for people will play an important part in determining the choices they make. And by deciding to participate in a certain location, they contribute to that place's community spirit.

APPENDIX A

Analysis of Various Aspects of Community by the Socioeconomic Characteristics of the Residents

This appendix presents an analysis of the following: utilization of neighborhood facilities, neighboring, organizational involvement, kin, friends, work, primary social relationships, and intimate emotional ties. The results presented in this section are first discussed in terms of the responses given by the total sample interviewed. Each of the questions is then analyzed separately for a number of different subgroups through the use of either crosstabulations or multiple regression analysis. When crosstabulations are employed, the sample is analyzed separately by age (18–34, 35–44, 45–54, 55–64, 65 and above); income ($7,000 and less, $7,001–13,000, $13,001–20,000, $20,001 and above); race (black and white); and household composition (married without children, married with children, separated/divorced without children, separated/divorced with children, widowed without children, widowed with children, and single). For each of these subgroups only statistically significant results are presented (chi square significant at 0.01 level). Multiple regression analysis is utilized to analyze differences in responses to the questions pertaining to use of neighborhood facilities and neighboring.

Utilization of Neighborhood Facilities

In order to examine the relationship between the use of neighborhood facilities and personal characteristics of the respondent, multiple regression analysis was employed. A neighborhood facilities use index was constructed by combining and weighting equally the respondent's answers to the five questions shown in Table 3. The index was then regressed upon the independent variables: age, income, family composition (number of people in the household and number of children under 18 years of age), race (black, white), length of residence in the neighborhood, and housing tenure (homeowner, renter). The results are shown in Table A-1.

Neighborhood facilities are used more frequently by higher-income residents, younger respondents, white respondents, renters, larger households, and those with longer tenure in the neighborhood. Part of the explanation for these results is the availability of these facilities among the respondents' neighborhoods. Availability was then controlled for by analyzing only the responses to the frequency-of-use questions for the respondents who reported that these facilities were available in or near the neighborhood. The analysis, excluding those without these facilities, showed that these facilities were still used more frequently by larger households, whites, and those living in the neighborhood for longer periods of time (see the analysis for Index 2 in Table A-1).

Neighboring

Multiple regression analysis was employed to analyze variations in neighboring activities among the respondents. A neighboring index was constructed by adding together and weighting equally the respondents' answers to the four neighboring questions shown in Table 4. The independent variables were the same as those used in the neighborhood facilities analysis. Neighboring occurred more frequently for smaller households, those with children, younger respondents, white respondents, higher-income households, homeowners, and those living in the neighborhood a longer time (Table A-1).

From a choice-constraint perspective, one would predict that those who are less mobile would neighbor with greater frequency than those who are less tied to the neighborhood. It is therefore

*Table A-1. Use of Neighborhood Facilities and Neighboring:
Multiple Regression Analysis*

Independent variables[a]	Use of neighborhood facilities		Neighboring index[d]
	Index 1[b]	Index 2[c]	
Number of people in household	.11	.14	−.06
Number of children in household	—	—	.16
Age of respondent	−.10	—	−.24
Household income	.08	—	.08
Nominal variable for race (black = 1, white = 0)	−.16	−.16	−.13
Nominal variable for homeownership (homeowner = 1, renter = 0)	−.04	—	.12
Length of residence in neighborhood	.13	.13	.06
N	4,063	2,201	3,777
R^2	.08	.07	.13

[a]Beta coefficients are shown for those variables significant at $p = 0.05$.
[b]The index was constructed by adding together and weighting equally the respondents' answers to each of the five questions shown in Table 3. The response categories were coded 1 (none) to 4 (all). Respondents who had previously stated that the facility was not available in the neighborhood were coded 1 (none).
[c]The index was constructed similar to Index 1 described above, except that the respondents who had previously stated that the facility was not available in the neighborhood were excluded from the analysis.
[d]The index was constructed by adding together and weighting equally the respondents's answers to each of the four questions shown in Table 4. The response categories were coded 1 (never) to 4 (often) and 0 (no) and 1 (yes).

not surprising that homeowners and households with children neighbor more. However, it is surprising that higher-income households neighbor with greater regularity since they have more opportunity to leave the neighborhood. Nonetheless, this result is consistent with other research,[1] and it may reflect a greater distrust by poor households of their neighbors, possibly emanating

[1]Kathleen Gerson, C. Ann Stueve, and Claude S. Fischer, "Attachment to Place," in *Networks and Places*, Claude S. Fischer *et al.*, pp. 139–61.

from higher incidences of reported and unreported crime in poorer neighborhoods than in those composed of higher-income households. The elderly tend to neighbor less, perhaps for some of the same reasons and also because they are less mobile even within their own neighborhood. The reason that black respondents neighbor less may be explained in part by differences in the characteristics of the neighborhoods they inhabit (poorer and more heterogeneous[2]) and also because they go outside of the neighborhood more frequently for shopping, churchgoing, and recreational activities.

Organizational Involvement

Organizational involvement was examined with respect to participation in organizations dealing with neighborhood issues and membership in other organizations, such as PTA, fraternal, union, little league, religious, and so on. Seventeen percent of the sample belong to at least one neighborhood issue organization, and 55% of the respondents are members of other voluntary organizations. Of these other organizations, the respondents' neighbors belong to 56%, and over half are located in or near the neighborhood. Viewed in another light, 35% of the total sample interviewed belong to other organizations which are located in or near the neighborhood, and 29% belong to one in which neighbors also participate.

The neighborhood therefore offers a variety of opportunities for participation. However, participation is not restricted to the place of residence. Of those who reported doing volunteer work during the past year, 56% spent all or most of their time on activities outside the neighborhood.

Age. The greatest amount of participation in organizations concerned with neighborhood issues is in the 35–44 age bracket, where almost one in four people belong to some local organization, compared to one in 10 in the 18–34 bracket and one in six in 65 years and above. Participation in other organizations is also greatest in the 35–44 bracket. Generally, the younger people par-

[2]Donald I. Warren makes the point that black neighborhoods are poorer and yet more heterogeneous than white areas. See his *Black Neighborhoods: An Assessment of Community Power* (Ann Arbor: University of Michigan Press, 1975).

ticipate in organizations outside the neighborhood to the greatest extent. Fifty-three percent of those in the 18–34 age group who belong to organizations participate in one located in or near the neighborhood, compared to 71% of those who participate in the 65-and-above age bracket. Similarly, those in the 18–34 age group spend less of their volunteer time on neighborhood-related activities than do the others.

Income. Participation in a neighborhood issue-related organization varies directly with income. Thirteen percent of those with annual household incomes of less than $7,000 per year belong to at least one local organization, compared to 23% with household incomes exceeding $20,000 per year. Participation in other voluntary organizations also directly varies with income. Forty-five percent of those with annual incomes less than $7,000 belong, compared to 66% of those with incomes exceeding $20,000 per year. The location of these other organizations also is dependent upon income. Higher-income people tend to belong to organizations located outside the neighborhood to a greater extent than lower-income respondents. Forty-three percent of participants with incomes above $20,000 belong to another organization located in the neighborhood, compared to 55% of those with incomes of less than $7,000.

Race. Black respondents belong to neighborhood issue organizations at a slightly higher rate than do white respondents (20% as opposed to 16%). There is no statistical difference in the rates of participation in other organizations; however, there is a small difference in the location of these organizations. Forty-five percent of the blacks who participate belong to one located in their neighborhood, compared to 50% of the whites.

Household Composition. Married couples belong to neighborhood issue organizations more often than do other kinds of households. Twenty-three percent of the married households with children belong, compared to a sample average of 17%. Households with children participate at higher rates than those headed by similar individuals (separated, divorced, widowed) without children, and respondents identifying themselves as single participate the least (10%). Membership in other organizations is also highest for married couples with children. Sixty-eight percent of these households belong, compared to a sample average of 55%. Similarly, households with children participate at higher rates than those that have no children. These other organizations are found in the neighborhood more frequently for households with children than for those without.

Kin in Neighborhood

Forty-four percent of the respondents have kin living in their neighborhood. This varies slightly by age group, income level, and family composition, but not by race. Fifty percent of those in the 45–54 age group report kin in their neighborhood, compared to 40% in both the 18–34 and 65-and-above age brackets. Forty percent of those with annual household income of less than $7,000 have kin living in the neighborhood, compared to slightly higher percentages for the other income groups. Households with children are more likely to have kin in the neighborhood than those without children, and respondents reporting themselves to be single are the least likely to have kin in the neighborhood.

Friends in Neighborhood

Seventy-five percent of the respondents report having at least one good friend in their neighborhood. The average respondent reports having 4.5 good friends living in the neighborhood. Older respondents had more friends than did younger respondents (5.6 for 65 and older compared to 3.4 for those in the 18–34 group). Households with children had fewer good friends than those without children. The fewest number of good friends was reported by separated/divorced households with children (3.3) and the most by married couples without children (5.5). There were no statistically significant differences found for this variable among race or income groups.

Work in Neighborhood

Approximately 20% of those who are currently attached to the labor force (working full time or part-time or unemployed) or are retired work or worked in or near their neighborhood (14% of the total sample). Part-time workers are employed in or near the neighborhood to a greater extent than the rest. Thirty percent of the men and 39% of the women working part-time do so in or near the neighborhood. Women in general work closer to home than men. Fourteen percent of men who are employed full time work in or near their neighborhood, compared to 24% for the full-time female family workers.

There are no large differences in the incidence of neighborhood jobs among age, income, or family composition groups. Those in the 65-and-older group work in the neighborhood at a slightly lower rate than the rest of the population (17% as opposed to 20%); those with incomes above $20,000 work outside the city to a greater extent than those in lower-income groups (19% compared to 11% for those under $7,000); and households with children work in the neighborhood at slightly higher rates than those without children.

Whites work in the neighborhood more often than blacks (21% of the whites compared to 15% of the blacks), but whites also work outside of the city to a greater extent than blacks (17% of the whites compared to 12% of the blacks).

Primary Social Relationships

The respondent was asked, "Among your friends, which person do you socialize with or visit most often?" Follow-up questions were asked to ascertain the relationship of this person to the respondent (relative, co-worker, etc.) and the place of residence (same neighborhood, in the city but outside the neighborhood, etc.). Ninety-five percent of those interviewed said they had a good friend with whom they socialized, and generally this person was other than a relative. Over half of the respondents said this person lived within their neighborhood.

Age. Age is directly related to the place of residence of the primary social contact. Forty-nine percent of the respondents in the 18–34 group report that this person lives in their neighborhood, compared to 62% of those in the 65-and-above age group.

Income. Lower-income respondents socialize more often with a person living in the neighborhood (63% for those in the lowest income group compared to 49% for those in the highest). The primary social contact lives outside of the city for 17% of those with incomes above $20,000 compared to 11% for those with incomes of less than $7,000.

Race. The primary social contact for blacks and whites lives in the neighborhood for 58% and 54%, respectively, of the respondents. The primary social contact lives outside of the city for 16% of the white respondents and 7% of the blacks interviewed.

Household Composition. Widows socialize more often with a neighborhood friend than do other respondents. Sixty-four percent of widows with children and 61% of those without children have their primary social contact living in the area. Married households have the next highest rate of neighborhood social friends (55% of households both with and without children). Approximately 50% of the single, separated, and divorced households have their primary social contact living in the neighborhood.

Intimate Ties

In order to assess intimate ties, respondents were asked, "When you do talk to someone about your personal concerns, with whom do you talk?" Seventy-two percent of those interviewed talk to at least one adult outside of their household, and 34% talk to at least two. Approximately 50% of these people were kin; almost a third lived within the respondents' neighborhood; and approximately 30% lived outside of the city (less than 10% lived outside of the state).

Age. Elderly people are less likely to turn to others to discuss personal matters. Thirty-three percent of those 65 and older reported that they seldom or never do, compared to 18% of those in the 18–34 age group. The elderly are more likely to rely upon kin for their emotional supports than are those in the youngest age group. Forty-one percent of the people mentioned by those in the 18–34 age group are kin, compared to 59% for those 65 and above. The elderly are also more likely to turn to people living within the neighborhood than are the younger respondents. Respondents 65 and above reported that 36% of their providers of emotional supports live within their neighborhood, compared to 28% for those in the 18–34 age group. Those 65 and older are less likely to rely upon people who live outside of the city than are those in the youngest age bracket.

Income. Lower-income respondents are less likely to talk over personal matters with someone than are those with higher income (11% of those with incomes of less than $7,000 report never, compared to 4% for respondents with incomes of $20,000 and above). Respondents in the highest income group are slightly more likely to call on a friend as opposed to kin for emotional supports than are the others. Higher-income groups are less likely to have the people they turn to living within the neighborhood and more likely to have these people residing outside of the city than are lower-income groups. Thirty percent of those in the $20,000 and above bracket, compared to 35% of the respondents with incomes below $7,000 per year, report that their primary provider of emotional supports lives in the neighborhood. Also, a higher percentage of the providers live outside of the city for those in the highest income bracket compared to those in the lowest.

Race. Black respondents are less likely to talk over emotional problems than are whites (29% never do or rarely, compared to 24% of the whites). Whites turn to kin slightly more often than do blacks, and whites are less likely to have the person they turn to living in the neighborhood and more likely to have the people residing outside of the city.

Household Composition. Widows are the least likely to talk over personal matters (approximately one-third report never or rarely). Married couples with children and single individuals are the most likely (approximately 80% report sometimes or often). Single individuals are the least likely to rely on kin for emotional supports (approximately 66% of the people mentioned are friends), and widows with no children are the most likely to rely on kin (approximately 60% are kin). Widowed households and separated/divorced households with children have the highest percentage of their providers of emotional supports living in the neighborhood, whereas single and separated/divorced households without children report the lowest percentages (widows with children report that 45% lived within the neighborhood, compared to 28% for separated/divorced households with no children). Single individuals and married couples without children report the highest percentages of their providers living outside of the city.

CHAPTER 3

Attitudes about Neighborhoods

INTRODUCTION

The choice-constraint model discussed in the previous chapter can be expanded to provide a framework in which to analyze people's feelings about their place of residence. Just as people's behavior is constrained by their socioeconomic circumstances, so is it constrained by the characteristics of the neighborhood in which they live. The neighborhood environment, through the quality of life it offers, the availability of services, and the fabric of its social life, *influences peoples' decisions* about participating in neighborhood activities and may directly affect the choices available to them. People living in a neighborhood which offers a variety of services—religious, recreational, shopping— have greater choice about where to engage in these activities than those living in places devoid of these services. People living in a neighborhood with a strong social fabric—a place in which significant interpersonal interaction occurs—have more opportunities to meet their social and emotional needs there than those living in neighborhoods where the social fabric is weak or nonexistent. Finally, those living in a neighborhood in which the quality of life is desirable, as evidenced by a low crime rate and safe, secure streets, have a greater incentive to go out and participate in neighborhood activities than those living in places where the fear of crime keeps people housebound.

These characteristics of the neighborhood environment may also reinforce one another in constructing a stronger or weaker community. For instance, a neighborhood that has many local services increases the opportunities for its residents to interact, and this contact may lead to a stronger social fabric. Or, a neighborhood with a high crime rate may discourage people from neighboring and as a result the fabric of its social life is weak.

The model which serves as the conceptual framework for the analysis of people's feelings about their neighborhood is shown in Figure 1. People's feelings about their place of residence are shown to be a function of the neighborhood's quality of life, its social fabric, and the characteristics of the other residents. As discussed above, some of these variables are interrelated. Certain characteristics of the residents may influence various dimensions of the social fabric and both of these variables may in turn affect, or be affected by, the quality of life in the neighborhood. For instance, the income level of the neighborhood (and surrounding neighborhoods) will influence the financial viability of a neighborhood shopping area, which in turn has a direct bearing on the availability and quality of the services provided. Or, the presence of a large Catholic pop-

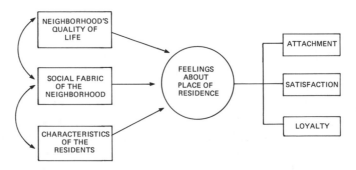

Figure 1. Modeling people's feelings about place of residence.

ulation in the neighborhood may support a neighborhood church which is then able to provide services to the parishioners, thereby raising the neighborhood's quality of life.

The model depicts a cause-and-effect relationship running from quality of life, social fabric, and resident characteristics to the variables that capture people's feelings about their neighborhood. The causal relationship between feelings and social fabric could run in the opposite direction. That is, people's feelings about their neighborhood, no matter how they arose, could affect their willingness to interact and therefore influence the strength of the neighborhood's social fabric. Given the cross-sectional nature of the research described in this book, it is not possible to observe the direction of this relationship. Although this is a limitation of the study, the relative importance of a number of discrete variables with respect to explaining differences in the feelings that people have about their neighborhood can be determined, and this by itself augments our understanding of the urban environment.

The relationships shown in Figure 1 are consistent with the literature. Ahlbrandt and Cunningham showed that residents' affective sentiments toward their neighborhood (their expressed commitment toward it and their satisfaction with it as a place to live) are associated with the social fabric of the neighborhood, the quality of life, the use of neighborhood facilities, the sense of community felt by the residents, and their satisfaction with their housing.[1] Gerson, Stueve, and Fischer analyzed attachment in terms of institutional ties, neighboring, organizational involvement, kin in neighborhood, and affective feelings (happiness with neighborhood and unhappiness if forced to move).[2] Kasarda and Janowitz analyzed community attachment with respect to number of friends, number of rela-

[1]Roger S. Ahlbrandt, Jr., and James V. Cunningham, *A New Public Policy for Neighborhood Preservation* (New York: Praeger, 1979).

[2]Kathleen Gerson, C. Ann Stueve, and Claude S. Fischer, "Attachment to Place," in *Networks and Places,* Claude S. Fischer *et al.* (New York: Free Press, 1977).

tives, formal organizational membership, participation in informal social activities, number of acquaintances, sense of community, and feelings about leaving the community.[3]

These studies illustrate that people's involvement in, attachment to, and feelings about their community have a number of discrete dimensions. Common to all of these studies are aspects of the formal and informal neighborhood ties and affective sentiments.[4]

AFFECTIVE SENTIMENTS

The affective sentiments of people toward their neighborhood were examined in the research through three general survey questions, which seek to capture feelings of attachment, satisfaction and loyalty.

1. *Attachment.* When you think of your attachment to this neighborhood, are you very strongly attached, strongly attached, undecided, not strongly attached, or not at all attached?
2. *Satisfaction.* In general, how would you rate this neighborhood as a place to live? Is it excellent, good, fair, or poor?
3. *Loyalty.* Does your neighborhood claim a greater loyalty from you than the rest of the city? (Yes, No)

The majority (63%) of Pittsburgh's residents report that they are strongly attached to their neighborhood, com-

[3]John D. Kasarda and Morris Janowitz, "Community Attachment in Mass Society," *American Sociological Review* 39 (June 1974): 328–39.

[4]Also see Angus Campbell, Philip E. Converse, and Willard L. Rodgers, *The Quality of American Life: Perceptions, Evaluations and Satisfaction* (New York: Russell Sage Foundation, 1977), Ch. 4; Albert Hunter, *Symbolic Communities* (Chicago: University of Chicago Press, 1974), Ch. 4; and Marc Fried and Peggy Gleicher, "Some Sources of Residential Satisfaction in an Urban Setting," in *Neighborhood, City and Metropolis,* ed. Robert Gutman and David Popenoe, (New York: Random House, 1970): 730–745.

Table 6. Affective Sentiments[a]

Question	Percentage of respondents
When you think of your attachment to this neighborhood, are you very strongly attached, strongly attached, undecided, not strongly attached, or not at all attached?	
(a) Very strongly	23
(b) Strongly	40
(c) Undecided	12
(d) Not strongly	18
(e) Not at all	7
In general, how would you rate this neighborhood as a place to live?	
(a) Excellent	24
(b) Good	48
(c) Fair	23
(d) Poor	5
Does your neighborhood claim a greater loyalty from you than the rest of the city?	
(a) Yes	63
(b) No	37

[a]Based on survey of neighborhood residents in city of Pittsburgh ($N = 5,896$).

pared to only 7% who report no attachment. A like percentage (63%) report greater loyalty to their neighborhood than to the city as a whole. Neighborhood satisfaction is also high. Seventy-two percent of all households interviewed rate their neighborhood a good or excellent place to live (See Table 6).

ANALYSIS

The relationships between respondents' sentiments and the independent variables, shown in Figure 1, describing quality of life, social fabric, and resident characteristics were investigated through multivariate statistical techniques. The basic model used for analytical purposes is shown in Equation 1:

$$(1) \qquad F = a_0 + a_1 Q + a_2 SF + a_3 RC + e$$

where F = feelings about the neighborhood; a_0 = constant term; $a_1 - a_3$ = coefficients; Q = neighborhood quality of life variables; SF = neighborhood social fabric variables; RC = characteristics of neighborhood residents; and e = error term. Although theoretically there could be potential interaction effects between the independent variables, the correlations between the variables are not high enough to make multicolinearity a significant concern. The correlation matrix for all of the variables used in the analysis is shown in Table 7.

Stepwise multiple regression analysis was used to examine the attachment- and satisfaction-dependent variables. Loyalty, being dichotomous, was analyzed through the use of discriminant function analysis. The same independent variables were used in all three cases, and they are listed below. A more detailed discussion of the variables is contained in Appendix B.

1. Quality of life variables
   a. Use of neighborhood facilities index
   b. Satisfaction with housing
   c. Satisfaction with public services
2. Social fabric variables
   a. Neighboring
   b. Relatives living in the neighborhood
   c. Number of good friends living in the neighborhood
   d. Place of residence of the person with whom the respondent socializes or visits most often
   e. Place of residence of the person with whom the respondent talks over his or her personal concerns
   f. Participation in neighborhood organizations

3. Respondent characteristics
   a. Number of children in the household
   b. Age
   c. Income
   d. Race
   e. Homeownership
   f. Length of residence in the neighborhood

DISCUSSION OF RESULTS

The results of the multiple regression analysis are shown in Table 8. The most important explanatory variables of attachment are length of residence in the neighborhood, use of neighborhood facilities, neighboring, age, and satisfaction with housing; they all relate positively to attachment. With respect to satisfaction, the primary explanatory variables, all positively related, are satisfaction with public services, satisfaction with housing, and income. It is interesting to note that the level of importance of the explanatory variables differs between the two equations and this stresses that attachment and satisfaction are two different feelings. Attachment is related more to the psychological commitment one has to the neighborhood (age, time lived in neighborhood), the fabric of the social life, and the uses that one makes of the neighborhood (shopping, churchgoing), while satisfaction is influenced more directly by the extent to which the services provided in the neighborhood (housing, public services) match the tastes, preferences, and needs of those living there. The differences between the sentiments of attachment and satisfaction are underscored by their moderate correlation (0.34), which is shown in Table 7.

The discriminant function analysis of the neighborhood loyalty question is shown in Table 9. For purposes of interpretation, the function relates directly to greater loyalty to the neighborhood. Thus, the higher a respondent's score, the greater the probability of his or her being clas-

Table 7. Correlation Matrix

Variable identification and description[a]	a	b	c	d	e	f	g	h	i	j	k	l	m	n	o	p	q	r
a. Use of neighborhood facilities index	1.00																	
b. Satisfaction with housing	.13	1.00																
c. Satisfaction with public services	.13	.20	1.00															
d. Neighboring index	.21	.12	.04	1.00														
e. Relatives in neighborhood (yes = 1; no = 0)	.16	.02	−.03	.08	1.00													
f. Number of good friends in neighborhood	.11	.08	.05	.18	.14	1.00												
g. Place of residence—social friend	.08	.04	−.01	.14	.11	.22	1.00											
h. Place of residence—emotional support provider	.04	−.01	−.04	.05	.19	.14	.19	1.00										

	a	b	c	d	e	f	g	h	i	j	k	l	m	n	o	p	q	r
i. Belonging to neighborhood organizations	.17	.09	-.02	.16	.09	.16	.11	.08	1.00									
j. Number of children in household	.13	-.04	.07	.17	.11	-.01	.03	.05	.14	1.00								
k. Age	-.12	.09	-.22	-.01	.13	.10	.07	.09	.09	-.30	1.00							
l. Household income	.16	.17	.06	.20	.01	-.04	-.10	-.07	.11	.19	-.30	1.00						
m. Race (black = 1; white = 0)	-.17	-.20	-.18	-.16	.01	-.02	.07	.10	.01	.04	.06	-.22	1.00					
n. Homeownership (homeowner = 1; renter = 0)	.05	.19	-.01	.13	.11	.08	.04	.05	.16	.18	.12	.04	-.15	1.00				
o. Length of residence in neighborhood	.10	.10	.13	-.04	.25	.20	.15	.13	.12	.23	.01	.25	.28	.29	1.00			
p. Attachment	.22	.21	.17	.17	.17	.20	.18	.14	.19	.19	.02	.17	-.08	-.02	.52	1.00		
q. Satisfaction	.22	.33	.34	.21	.02	.10	.05	.01	.10	.10	-.01	.21	-.25	.01	.23	.32	1.00	
r. Loyalty	.17	.11	.05	.11	.11	.10	.11	.08	.13	.13	.09	.11	-.02	.13	.09	.19	.42	1.00

aFor a more detailed description of the coding of these variables, see Table 8; variables are in same order going across and down the table.

Table 8. Affective Sentiments: Stepwise Multiple Regression Analysis

Independent variables[a]	Dependent variables	
	Attachment to neighborhood[b]	Satisfaction with neighborhood[c]
Neighborhood environment		
Use of neighborhood facilities (Index 1)[d]	15 (2)	.10 (6)
Satisfaction with housing[e]	.12 (3)	.19 (2)
Satisfaction with public services[f]	.06 (11)	.25 (1)
Social fabric		
Neighboring index[g]	.13 (4)	.10 (4)
Relatives living in the neighborhood (yes = 1; no = 0)	.05 (9)	— (15)
Number of good friends living in neighborhood	.05 (13)	.03 (11)
Place of residence of primary social friend[h]	.07 (6)	.03 (8)
Place of residence of primary provider of emotional supports[i]	.05 (8)	— (13)
Belonging to neighborhood organizations[j]	.06 (7)	— (12)
Respondent characteristics		
Number of children in household	— (15)	— (14)
Age of respondent	.13 (5)	.07 (7)
Household income	— (14)	.14 (3)
Nominal variable for race (black = 1; white = 0)	.07 (10)	−.11 (5)
Nominal variable for homeownership (homeowner = 1; renter = 0)	.05 (12)	.04 (10)
Length of residence in neighborhood	.19 (1)	−.06 (9)
N	3,896	3,896
R^2	.23	.26

[a] Beta coefficients are shown for those variables significant at $p = 0.05$; see the text for a detailed description of the independent variables.

[b] The survey question was scored 1 (not at all attached) to 4 (very strongly attached); high values connote increased attachment. The number in parentheses indicates the order in which the variables were entered into the equation.

[c] The survey question was scored 1 (poor) to 4 (excellent); high values show increased satisfaction. The number in parentheses indicates the order in which the variables were entered into the equation.

[d] Higher values connote greater use of neighborhood facilities.

[e] The survey question was scored 1 (very dissatisfied) to 5 (very satisfied); higher values show greater satisfaction.

[f] The survey question was scored 1 (very dissatisfied) to 5 (very satisfied); higher values show greater satisfaction.

[g] Higher values show increased neighboring.

[h] The survey question was scored 1 (outside of Pennsylvania) to 5 (in or near your neighborhood); higher values show closer proximity to the respondent.

[i] See note above for coding.

[j] The index was scored 0 (none) to 2 (belonging to at least two organizations located in or near the neighborhood); higher values show greater involvement.

Table 9. *Neighborhood Loyalty: Discriminant Function Analysis*

Description of the variables	Standardized discriminant coefficient[a]
Neighborhood environment	
Use of neighborhood facilities (Index 1)[b]	.43
Satisfaction with housing[c]	.17
Satisfaction with public services[d]	.13
Social fabric	
Neighboring index[e]	.22
Relatives living in the neighborhood (Yes = 1; No = 0)	.06
Number of good friends living in neighborhood	.03
Place of residence of primary social friend[f]	.12
Place of residence of primary provider of emotional supports[g]	.16
Belonging to neighborhood organizations[h]	.09
Respondent characteristics	
Number of children in household	−.06
Age of respondent	.06
Household income	.07
Nominal variable for race (black = 1; white = 0)	.16
Nominal variable for homeownership (homeowner = 1; renter = 0)	.15
Length of residence in neighborhood	.58

[a]The classification function is derived in terms of those who have greater loyalty to the neighborhood than to the city. Therefore, the higher a respondent's score, the greater the probability of that person's being classified as having greater loyalty to the neighborhood. The canonical correlation is 0.31; 63% of the cases were classified correctly; $N = 3,402$.
[b]Higher values connote greater use of neighborhood facilities.
[c]The survey question was scored 1 (very dissatisfied) to 5 (very satisfied); higher values show greater satisfaction.
[d]The survey question was scored 1 (very dissatisfied) to 5 (very satisfied); higher values show greater satisfaction.
[e]Higher values show increased neighboring.
[f]The survey question was scored 1 (outside of Pennsylvania) to 5 (in or near your neighborhood); higher values show closer proximity to the respondent.
[g]See note above for coding.
[h]The index was scored 0 (none) to 2 (belonging to at least two organizations located in or near the neighborhood); higher values show greater involvement.

sified as having greater loyalty to the neighborhood than to the city. The results closely parallel those of the attachment multiple regression. The three most important variables discriminating between those who have greater loyalty to the city than to the neighborhood are length of time in the neighborhood, use of neighborhood facilities, and neighboring. The age variable is not as important an explanatory variable for loyalty as it is for attachment, and the place of residence of the primary social contact and the provider of emotional supports variables are slightly more important for loyalty than they are for attachment. Given these results, it is not surprising that there is a much stronger correlation between the responses to the loyalty and attachment survey questions (0.42) than there is between the loyalty and satisfaction questions (0.21) (see Table 7).

Quality of Life

The use of neighborhood facilities is the second most important explanatory variable for both attachment and loyalty, but it is of only moderate importance for satisfaction.

Satisfaction with housing and satisfaction with public services are the two most important explanatory variables in the satisfaction regression, but they are of lesser importance for the other two sentiments.

It is difficult to interpret the implications of the significance of the housing and public services variables. The cause-and-effect relationship between these variables and the dependent variable could run both ways. Increased satisfaction with housing or the public services delivered to the neighborhood could lead to greater overall neighborhood satisfaction, high levels of attachment, and greater loyalty; or attachment, loyalty, and neighborhood satisfaction, for whatever the reasons, could lead to higher satisfaction with the housing and the public services. Despite this limitation, the inclusion of these variables in the analysis is important in order to increase the explanatory power of the equations and to attempt to hold constant neighborhood effects which otherwise might be picked up by the other independent variables.

Social Fabric

The social fabric variables are relatively more important explanatory variables for attachment and loyalty than they are for neighborhood satisfaction. This suggests that the social fabric that exists in an area can tie people to the neighborhood in a way which is different from, or somewhat independent of, their evaluation of the area as a place to live.

Participation in neighborhood organizations is a statistically significant explanatory variable for attachment but not for satisfaction.

Respondent Characteristics

Length of time lived in the neighborhood is the most important explanatory variable for both attachment and loyalty. Longer-term residents are more attached and are more loyal than shorter-term residents. Length of residence is statistically significant in the satisfaction equation, but it is not one of the more important explanatory variables. It does, however, vary inversely with satisfaction. Respondents who have lived in the neighborhood for longer periods of time are less satisfied. This could reflect changing needs and expectations on the part of neighborhood residents. Those who most recently moved into the neighborhood did so because that location, out of all possible alternatives, best met their needs. The preferences of longer-term residents, however, may have altered with respect to the type of neighborhood in which they would choose to live, but because of their psychological attachment to the neighborhood, they may be reluctant to move.

Older respondents are more attached and loyal to the

neighborhood and more satisfied with it as a place to live. Greater attachment and loyalty may result from their having less opportunity to go out of the neighborhood and thus being more dependent upon it, whereas the higher levels of satisfaction may be a result of either the fact that their needs are being met to a greater extent than other respondents (unlikely) or the fact that their expectations are lower (more likely).

Income is not a statistically significant explanatory variable for attachment (not very important for loyalty either), but it is for satisfaction. Higher satisfaction levels are directly related to increased income. This is not surprising because higher-income households have the opportunity to select their place of residence from among a larger group of neighborhoods than do households with less income and therefore should be able to choose the location that best matches their tastes and preferences; higher-income households are less dependent upon the neighborhood and have the financial resources to relocate if they become dissatisfied with the neighborhood and the services provided.

Black households are more attached and more loyal, but they are less satisfied. This may reflect the fact that blacks have fewer opportunities to relocate out of the neighborhood, and hence the greater attachment, but they are less satisfied because service levels are inferior or at least their expectations are not being met to as great an extent as are the expectations of white respondents.

Homeowners are more satisfied and report greater attachment than renters. The higher satisfaction may reflect more thought on the part of homeowners with respect to matching their needs to the neighborhood because of their greater financial stake in the area compared to renters who are more mobile. Also, just the fact of being a homeowner may lead to greater satisfaction. For similar reasons, greater attachment may be a result of the significant financial stake in the neighborhood, which may lead to a greater psychological commitment to the area for homeowners as well.

When all other variables are controlled for, the number of children in the household is not a statistically significant variable in the attachment and satisfaction equations, nor is it a very important discriminating variable for neighborhood loyalty.

CONCLUSION

The analysis shows that various dimensions of the neighborhood environment, as well as the characteristics of the residents, influence the feelings that people have about their place of residence. The neighborhood constrains people's choices in the sense that it affects their opportunities for participation and interaction. Therefore, given the choice of participating within the neighborhood or within the greater community, people's decisions will depend to some extent upon the ability of the neighborhood to meet their needs. The neighborhood, therefore, can draw people inward if it offers people the opportunity to engage in activities and if its quality of life does not discourage participation.

Residents themselves can also play a role in constructing their community. This is evident by the importance of the social fabric variables in the attachment and loyalty equations. It is the interaction among the residents that builds the fabric of the social life, and it is this facet of the community which has an important influence on people's commitment toward it.

This chapter also shows that there are differences among the factors associated with people's affective sentiments toward their neighborhood. Feelings of attachment and loyalty capture many of the same dimensions but they vary in some respects as well. Both of these variables, however, differ significantly from the respondents' ratings of the neighborhood as a place to live.

The institutional structure of the neighborhood, in terms of facilities for shopping, worship, and voluntary organizations, is shown to be relatively more important for attachment and loyalty than it is for satisfaction. The social fabric of the neighborhood also appears to be relatively more significant for the feelings of attachment and loyalty than it is for neighborhood satisfaction.

Although the social fabric of the neighborhood may be somewhat elusive, it is an important concept to understand because it provides the context in which people live on a daily basis and it contributes to the overall quality of life within the neighborhood. This chapter has shown that the fabric of the social and institutional relationships within a neighborhood are related in a significant way to the feelings people have toward their place of residence. Therefore, the communal nature of a neighborhood is influenced by the strength of the social relationships which exist and the availability and quality of neighborhood-based institutions.

APPENDIX B

Description of the Independent Variables

This appendix describes the independent variables used in the multivariate analysis.

Quality of Life Variables

The neighborhood's quality of life was described by an index which captured the extent to which residents used neighborhood facilities, reported satisfaction with housing, and described their satisfaction with public services in the neighborhood. Each of these variables is described in more detail below. The research did not gather any data to measure objectively the quality of life in the neighborhood; instead, various proxies, collected in the resident survey, were used. The use of satisfaction variables as proxies for various dimensions of the quality of life may introduce problems in the interpretation of the results if there is no systematic relationship between people's attitudes about their housing and their actual housing conditions, or if there is no consistent relationship between satisfaction with public services and the actual quality of the services provided. It was not possible to assess the extent to which this may have been a problem in the research.

Use of Neighborhood Facilities Index. This index was constructed by adding together and weighting equally the respondents' answers to the question, "How often do you _____ in or near your neighborhood [(1) shop for groceries, (2) shop for small items, (3) attend church or religious services, (4) use health facilities, and (5) use recreation facilities]?" The response categories were none, some, most or all of the time. This variable is a proxy for both the availability of services in the neighborhood and the quality of the services provided (presumably if the quality is poor, the respondent will go elsewhere). It was assumed that the greater the use of facilities in the neighborhood, the more attached, loyal, and satisfied would be the respondent.

Satisfaction with Housing. Satisfaction with housing was obtained from answers to the question, "How would you rate the home/apartment in meeting the needs of you and your family? Are you very satisfied, satisfied, neither satisfied nor dissatisfied, dissatisfied, or very dissatisfied?" It was assumed that greater satisfaction represented a higher quality of living unit. This variable was expected to relate directly to attachment, loyalty, and satisfaction.

Satisfaction with Public Services. Satisfaction with public services was obtained from answers to the question, "In general, how satisfied are you with the way the city provides services in this neighborhood? Are you very satisfied, satisfied, neither satisfied nor dissatisfied, dissatisfied, or very dissatisfied?" It was assumed that greater satisfaction related, at least in the minds of the respondents, to better public services. Greater satisfaction with neighborhood public services was expected to lead to higher levels of attachment and loyalty and increased neighborhood satisfaction.

Social Fabric Variables

The social fabric of the neighborhood was considered to be multidimensional and was portrayed by the following variables: a neighboring activities index; whether or not the respondent had relatives living in the neighborhood; the number of good friends living in the neighborhood; the place of residence of the person with whom the respondent socialized most often; the place of residence of the person on whom the respondent relied for emotional supports; and the involvement of the respondent in voluntary organizations located in or near the neighborhood. Each of these is described below.

Neighboring. A neighboring index was constructed by adding together and weighting equally the respondents' answers to the four questions: (1) "How often do you borrow from or exchange things with your neighbors?"; (2) "How often do you visit with your neighbors?"; (3) "Within the past year, how often have people in this neighborhood helped you or you helped them with small tasks such as repair work or grocery shopping?''; and (4) "If an emergency arose in your home such as an accident requiring assistance of adults, could you call on your neighbors for help?'' Response categories for the first three questions were never, rarely, sometimes, or often; for the fourth question the categories were yes and no. It was assumed that neighboring would relate directly to attachment, loyalty and satisfaction.

Relatives in the Neighborhood. "Do you have relatives living in this neighborhood?" (Yes/No)

Number of Good Friends Living in the Neighborhood. Actual number of friends.

Place of Residence of the Person with Whom the Respondent Socializes or Visits Most Often. The respondent was asked to identify the place of residence, and the responses were coded on a five-point scale, from one (outside of Pennsylvania) to five (in your neighborhood—say within a 10-minute walk of your home). It was hypothesized that attachment, loyalty, and satisfaction would vary directly with the nearness of the friend.

Place of Residence of the Person with Whom the Respondent Talks over His or Her Personal Concerns. The question was coded as described above and the same direction of the relationship between location and attachment, loyalty, and satisfaction was assumed.

Involvement in Neighborhood Organizations. This variable is an index which includes answers to the questions of whether or not the respondent participates in any organization or group in the neighborhood that deals with neighborhood issues or neighborhood problems, and any other organization, such as a church group, PTA, fraternal, union, or little league, which is located in or near the neighborhood. The rationale behind this index is that participation provides the individual with an opportunity to become more involved in the neighborhood and to make friends. This variable should therefore relate directly to attachment, loyalty, and satisfaction.

Respondent Characteristics

The characteristics of the respondents were represented by the variables listed below.

Number of Children in the Household. Households with children should be more constrained geographically; they may be more dependent upon the neighborhood and therefore more attached and loyal to it. Since children spend more time in and around the neighborhood, these households may be expected to be more satisfied with it as a place to live than are other types of households.

Age of Respondent. Older households, because they lack the mobility of younger households, are more dependent upon the neighborhood. Therefore, age should be directly related to attachment, loyalty, and satisfaction.

Income. High-income households have greater mobility than those with less income; therefore, they should be less dependent upon the neighborhood and less attached and loyal to it. They may be more satisfied with the neighborhood, however, than lower-income residents because their choices of where to live are greater.

Race. The literature generally shows that blacks are less satisfied with their place of residence than whites.[1] With respect to attachment and loyalty, it is not obvious how the racial variable should relate.

Homeownership. Because of the greater financial investment in the neighborhood, homeowners were posited to be more attached, more loyal, and more satisfied than renters.

Length of Residence in Neighborhood. Longer-term residents may be expected to have a greater psychological investment in the neighborhood; their attachment and loyalty should therefore be greater. They may or may not be more satisfied. On the one hand, because they have lived there longer, it would seem that they should be more satisfied because they have decided not to move.

---

[1]For examples see Hunter (1974), Ch. 4; Joel D. Aberbach and Jack L. Walker, "The Attitudes of Blacks and Whites Toward City Services: Implications for Public Policy," in *Financing the Metropolis,* ed. John P. Crecine (Beverly Hills, Calif.: Sage, 1970); Floyd Fowler, *Citizen Attitudes Toward Local Government, Services and Taxes* (Cambridge, Mass.: Ballinger, 1974); Nicholas P. Lovrich, Jr., and G. Thomas Taylor, Jr., "Neighborhood Evaluation of Local Government Services," *Urban Affairs Quarterly* 12 (December 1976): 197–222; and Howard Schuman and Barry Gruenberg, "Dissatisfaction with City Services: Is Race an Important Factor?" in *People and Politics in Urban Society,* ed. Harlan Hahn (Beverly Hills, Calif.: Sage, 1971).

But, because they have a greater psychological commitment to their place of residence, the psychological costs of a move are higher and therefore they may elect to stay, up to a point, even if they are not very satisfied with conditions in the neighborhood.

CHAPTER 4

Religion, Life Cycle, and Race

INTRODUCTION

The neighborhood offers its residents opportunities to interact and to build a sound community. Whether the people choose to do so depends upon the choices and constraints they face, and as the previous chapter showed, the neighborhood plays an important role in helping to create a sense of community. The neighborhood can pull people inward if the services that it offers are relatively attractive, and conversely it can push people outward and discourage the construction of community if the various aspects of the neighborhood environment do not meet the needs, wants, or desires of the residents. It is therefore not only the interaction among the residents that gives rise to the feelings that people have about place, but it is also the interplay between the residents and the neighborhood itself. If the neighborhood pulls people inward by meeting many of their needs, then feelings of attachment, loyalty, and commitment will be stronger than if the residents elect to go outside of their neighborhood to satisfy many of their desires because the services and amenities offered by the neighborhood are relatively inferior. This chapter examines the interaction between the neighborhood and the residents in more detail to ascertain how the push and pull of the neighborhood works among different groups of people.

REASONS FOR MOVING TO THE NEIGHBORHOOD

The single most important reason for moving into the neighborhood is convenience, given by 24% of the respondents; however, having been born in the neighborhood or having friends, family, or spouse living there combine to represent 38% of the total number of responses (Table 10). This is an indication of the strength and importance of the social fabric of the neighborhood. People live there because they have ties there. Housing is also important, cited by 10% of the respondents.

There were no significant differences in the reasons given for moving into the neighborhood within age, income, and family composition groups except that younger respondents (18–34), single respondents, and higher-income respondents ($20,000 and above) all placed more emphasis on convenience (exceeding 30% of the total number of respondents in each category). In addition, single parent households with children placed more emphasis on reasonable housing prices than did the sample as a

Table 10. Reasons for Moving into the Neighborhood

Reason	Total responses (in percentages)		
	Whites	Blacks	Total
Convenient location	26	18	24
Born and raised there	23	13	21
Friends, family, spouse lived there	17	15	17
Better neighborhood	10	15	11
Reasonably priced housing	8	15	10
Better home	6	8	6
Good schools	3	1	3
Safe neighborhood	1	1	1
Other	6	14	7
	100	100	100

Source: 1980 Citizen Survey.

whole (15% for separated and divorced households with children; 21% for widowed households with children).

A comparison of racial differences·shows great dissimilarity in the reasons people gave for moving into the neighborhood. Whites emphasized convenience to a greater degree than did blacks (26% versus 18%), and being born or having family ties in the neighborhood was much more important for whites than it was for blacks (40% and 28%). Black respondents stressed reasons related to housing (23%, 14% for whites) and the general neighborhood environment (16% versus 11%).

A profile of the characteristics of the residents and their reasons for moving into the neighborhood is shown in Table 11. Whites and Catholics were drawn into the neighborhood originally either because they had been born there or because they had more neighborhood ties with friends and family than did blacks and other religious groups. This may be a result of the length of time that different ethnic groups have lived in Pittsburgh's neighborhoods. On the average, blacks have lived in their neighborhood a shorter period of time than whites have (19 years versus 22 years), and Catholics have lived there longer than either Protestants or Jews (25 years compared to 20 years for Protestants and 18 for Jews).

The differences between the reasons given by blacks and whites for moving into the neighborhood are revealing. Blacks are less likely to be living in the neighborhood in which they were born, and they are more likely to have picked their current neighborhood because of its amenities and physical features, including affordable housing. The pull of the neighborhood on blacks is caused less by social and family ties and more by the improvement of the environment and housing over the areas where they had lived before. This may be a consequence of past and perhaps present housing market discrimination. To the extent that blacks have been denied equal access to housing and neighborhoods, it is understandable that when given the opportunity to move they would place greater emphasis on

*Table 11. Respondents' Characteristics and the Reasons Why
They Moved into the Neighborhood*

Characteristics of the respondents	Reason for moving into the neighborhood (in percentages)[a]		
	Amenities, physical features	Convenience	People
Relatives in the neighborhood	33	26	67
Best social friend in neighborhood	53	48	61
Person closest to in neighborhood	27	27	40
Strongly attached to the neighborhood	57	56	75
Rate neighborhood good or excellent	72	76	72
Homeownership	64	53	71
Black	28	17	16
Catholic	41	40	59
Mean household income	$14,910	$14,850	$12,480
Mean years lived in neighborhood	15	14	33

[a]Respondents were asked to state the reason they moved into the neighborhood. The following responses are included in the categories listed in the table: (a) amenities, physical facilities: safe neighborhood, good place to raise kids, good public services, good schools, better home (apartment), reasonable housing prices, better neighborhood, nice neighborhood; (b) convenience: good location, convenient; (c) people: friends lived here, family lived here, spouse lived here, born and raised here.

the physical features of the neighborhood and its housing stock than would whites. This finding is consistent with that of Chapter 3, which showed that blacks were less satisfied with their neighborhood than whites, even controlling for income differences. Limiting the choice of blacks implies that a greater percentage would be less happy with their current living conditions because they had fewer options among which to choose.

The findings present a different picture for Catholics.

Catholic neighborhoods show strong drawing power because of social factors. Almost half of all Catholic respondents moved into their neighborhood because they had been born there or had family or friends living there, and as Table 11 shows, Catholics represent about 60% of the respondents who were attracted to their neighborhood because of the people living there. The implications of this are discussed in later chapters.

Attachment to the neighborhood is stronger for those who were born in the neighborhood or moved into it for reasons of family, friends, or spouse. This sheds some light on the importance of the social fabric variables identified in the previous chapter as explanatory variables for loyalty and attachment. It is reasonable to expect that neighboring, number of friends in the neighborhood, and the like are stronger for those who moved into the neighborhood originally for reasons related to the presence of an established social support system within the neighborhood. Table 11 shows this to be the case. Respondents who reported people as the principal reason for moving into the neighborhood are more likely to have relatives, best social friend, and provider of emotional support living there, and they express higher levels of neighborhood attachment than other respondents. One of the results of this strong internal social fabric is significantly less resident turnover. Households who move into neighborhoods because of personal ties have lived there an average of 33 years, greater than twice that of households moving into neighborhoods for other reasons.

THINGS LIKED BEST ABOUT THE NEIGHBORHOOD

The location and the people were the two facets of the neighborhood most liked by the respondents in this study, being mentioned respectively, by 35% and 29% of the respondents. There were no significant differences among age groups. Lower-income respondents cited the residents at a slightly higher rate than did upper-income groups (31% of those with incomes less than $7,000 compared to 27% for those with incomes above $20,000). Upper-income groups mentioned location more frequently than did lower-income respondents (38% and 32% respectively for those with incomes above $20,000 and below $7,000). Blacks mentioned the security of the neighborhood at a higher rate than whites mentioned it (23% and 14%); and whites gave location as a reason more often than did blacks (36% and 29%). Jewish respondents mentioned location most frequently (48%; this compared to approximately one-third of the responses for Catholics and Protestants). Catholics mentioned people more often than other religious groups did (32% compared to 27% and 21% respectively for Protestant and Jewish respondents), and slightly in excess of half of the respondents who mentioned people were Catholics.

As shown in Table 12, the reasons people like their neighborhood varied to some extent among the different groups surveyed. Location and general satisfaction were mentioned most frequently by those groups that have the greatest economic mobility. As might be expected from their reasons for moving into the neighborhood, Catholics placed more emphasis on the people living in the neighborhood than did the other religious groups, and blacks were more likely to emphasize the amenities and physical features of the neighborhood. People who reported that they liked nothing about the neighborhood were more likely to be black and of low income than were other respondents. These individuals were also the least likely to have a personal support network in the neighborhood, and they were less satisfied and less attached to the neighborhood than were other respondents.

Those who expressed higher levels of attachment to the neighborhood reported that they were generally satisfied with the neighborhood or that the people were the aspect of the neighborhood that they liked the best. These individuals were more likely to have personal ties within

Table 12. Respondents' Characteristics and What They Like Best about Their Neighborhood

Characteristics of the respondents	What respondents like best about neighborhood (in percentages)[a]				
	Nothing	General satisfaction	Amenities, physical facilities	Convenience	People
Relatives in neighborhood	45	45	39	40	53
Best social friend in neighborhood	42	54	52	51	64
Person closest to in neighborhood	26	37	29	28	39
Strongly attached to neighborhood	23	74	57	59	78
Rate neighborhood good or excellent	21	82	74	70	78
Homeownership	53	70	63	56	70
Black	35	18	28	16	20
Catholic	46	48	43	45	53
Mean household income	$9,080	$14,470	$12,500	$14,390	$12,940
Mean years lived in neighborhood	21	25	19	19	25

[a]Respondents were asked, "What is the one thing about this neighborhood that you like best?" The following responses are included in the categories listed in the titles: (a) nothing: nothing; (b) general satisfaction: general satisfaction, the neighborhood; (c) amenities, physical facilities: home (apartment), cost of housing, well-maintained homes, quiet, private, small, clean, view, security, recreational facilities, stores, transportation; (d) convenience: convenience, location; (e) people: people, children-oriented.

the neighborhood than were the others. This underscores the social dimension of the neighborhood environment as being one of the critical factors in bonding people to their place of residence.

THINGS LIKED LEAST ABOUT THE NEIGHBORHOOD

Respondents were asked to identify the most serious problem in their neighborhood. Responses covered a wide

variety of problems; crime (15%), street repair and maintenance (11%), traffic and parking (11%), litter and garbage (10%), housing-related (8%), and youth-related (8%)
were the most frequently mentioned. Fifteen percent of the
respondents were not concerned about any problem in
their neighborhood.

The problems mentioned varied slightly among age
groups. Those 65 years of age and older were more concerned with safety than were the other age groups (18%
said it was the primary problem); but 24% of the elderly
reported that there was no major problem in their neighborhood—the highest response rate of any group. Traffic
problems were relatively more important for the younger
age groups. Those in the lowest income group reported
slightly higher rates of no problem (20%), safety (16%),
and litter and garbage (12%) than did the other groups.
Problems with traffic and sidewalk repair were more of a
concern to the higher-income groups. Whites felt there was
no problem a little more often than blacks did (16% versus
13%) and were more concerned than blacks about safety
(15% and 12%), sidewalk repair (12% and 6%), and traffic
(13% and 4%). Blacks were more concerned than whites
about litter and garbage (15% and 9%) and housing-related
problems (15% and 7%). A breakdown of respondents by
religion generally follows the black–white dichotomy, with
the responses of Protestants being similar to those of
blacks and the responses of the other religious groups corresponding to those of the whites.

The responses with respect to specific neighborhood
conditions vary in predictable patterns based upon the
analysis in Chapter 3. Higher-income respondents are less
likely to rate conditions in the neighborhood a problem
than are lower-income persons. Blacks are more likely to
rate conditions a problem than are whites. Age, however,
is not a good predictor across the board. Older people are
more concerned about problems related to their safety than
are younger ones, but older respondents are not so concerned about other conditions in the neighborhood.

Higher levels of attachment and neighborhood satis-faction, as would be expected, relate to more positive per-ceptions of conditions in the neighborhood. In addition, of those who are very strongly attached to the neighborhood, only 6% cite undesirable people as a major problem in the neighborhood, compared to 22% of those who state that they are not at all attached to the neighborhood; and of those who give the neighborhood an excellent rating, only 2% think that undesirable people in the neighborhood are a major problem, compared to 42% of those who rate the neighborhood a poor place to live.

Neighborhood problems and their perceived severity vary by the characteristics of the respondents. The higher level of dissatisfaction with neighborhood conditions expressed by blacks is entirely consistent with the argu-ment that blacks may not have had the opportunity to sat-isfy their housing and neighborhood choices to the same extent as whites. Lower incomes and housing market dis-crimination impose barriers that combine to diminish the mobility of black households.

The positive relationships between people's percep-tions of the neighborhood and their attitude about other people living there is further evidence of the role played by the social fabric of the neighborhood in the creation of community. Those who are dissatisfied with the neighbor-hood and those who have less attachment to it express the greatest concern about undesirable people living in the neighborhood.

PLANNING TO REMAIN IN THE NEIGHBORHOOD

Twenty-three percent of the respondents indicated that they planned to move within the next two years. This intent varied inversely with age. Forty-nine percent of those between 18 and 34 years of age planned to move, compared to 11% of those 65 and above. There was no statistically significant difference among income groups. Blacks reported that they planned to move slightly more often than whites did (28% versus 23%). Protestants indicated a greater likelihood of moving than did respondents of other religious groups (25%, as opposed to 20% for Catholic and Jewish respondents). In terms of household composition, 45% of the single individuals said they planned to move (they accounted for 39% of the planned moves), compared to 39% of the separated and divorced households with children and 30% of the widowed households with children. Fewer than 20% of the married households planned to move.

Of those planning to move, 23% indicated that they will remain within their neighborhood, 29% will relocate to another neighborhood in the city, 17% will move to a suburb in Allegheny County, 7% plan to live outside of Allegheny County, and 24% anticipate moving outside of Pennsylvania entirely.

The location of the anticipated move varies with age. Plans to move out of the state were reported more frequently by younger respondents than by older ones (70% of the anticipated moves out of Pennsylvania were by respondents in the 18–34 age group). Of those who intended to move, more than 60% of persons 45 and older, compared to only 45% of those under 45, planned to stay within the city.

The location of the move varied slightly by the respondent's income. Approximately 57% of those with incomes less than $7,000 intended to move either within the city or within their neighborhood, compared to 49% of those in the highest income category. Race was also a factor. Seventy-one percent of the black potential movers said they would move within the city or within their neighborhood, compared to 47% of the white potential movers. Among the religious groups, Catholics were most likely to move within the neighborhood (27% compared to 19% for Protestants and 22% for Jews), and they were least likely to move out of the state (17% compared to 25% for Protestants and 36% for Jews). The greatest incidence of planned moves outside of the state occurred among single individuals. Fifty-five percent of those planning to move outside of the state were single—this was 34% of the moves planned by this group. Married households with children had the highest rate of planned suburban moves (28%), and separated and divorced households with children had the highest rates of planned moves within the neighborhood (approximately 38%).

The socioeconomic data support a number of the hypotheses of the choice-constraint model of human behavior. Responses to the survey question (planning to move) by older respondents, by those with less income, and by those with family responsibilities, indicate that these individuals are less mobile than other respondents.

The primary reasons given for an anticipated move were as follows: finding a better place to live (23%); finding a larger home or apartment (15%); job transfer (12%); school-related (10%); purchasing a home (9%); retirement (5%); declining neighborhood conditions (4%); marriage or divorce (3%); and high rent (3%). These reasons varied significantly with age, income, race, and family composition. For instance, 87% of the job transfers, 83% of the home-buying, and 95% of the school-related reasons were given by respondents within the 18–34 age group, whereas retirement was concentrated in the older age groups (not too surprising). Job transfers increased with income (6% of the responses given by the lowest income group compared to 16% of the highest); and about half of the school-related responses were concentrated in the lowest income group. Whites expected to have a higher rate of job transfers than blacks (14% versus 5%); whites gave more school-related responses than blacks (13% and 4%); and blacks were more concerned about finding a better home or apartment than whites (35% and 19%). Single respondents accounted for almost 60% of the job transfers and 68% of the school-related responses. Housing reasons were given by most household types as the primary reason for the move.

Planning to move is related to the characteristics of the respondents and to changes in their stage of life cycle (marriage, retirement) as well as to a desire on the part of the respondents to change and/or improve their housing. The decision of respondents to stay in or move out of their neighborhood is also related to their affective sentiments toward their place of residence. The correlations between the survey question on planning to move and the feelings of neighborhood attachment and satisfaction are 0.31 and 0.22, respectively (these are statistically significant at $p = 0.01$ and indicate that those who plan to stay are more attached to the neighborhood and have higher satisfaction levels). Even though these correlations are not high, they nevertheless indicate that people's affective sentiments toward their neighborhood influence planned behavior.

Additional Analysis

Planning to move was further investigated through the use of discriminant function analysis. The same discriminating variables were used here as were employed in the analyses described in Chapter 3. The discriminant function shown in Table 13 was estimated for those who planned to stay in the neighborhood.

The results are not surprising given the discussion in the preceding pages. The most important variables discriminating between those who plan to move and those who do not are age, homeownership, and satisfaction with housing. Older respondents, homeowners, and people who are satisfied with their housing are less likely to move than are the others. The next group of discriminating variables, in terms of importance, includes the number of children in the household, neighboring, use of neighborhood facilities, and relatives in the neighborhood. Households with children are less likely to move. Similarly, those who engage more in neighboring activities, use neighborhood facilities more frequently, and have relatives living in the neighborhood also indicate that they are less likely to move.

Table 13. Planning to Move: Discriminant Function Analysis

Description of the variable	Standardized discriminant coefficient[a]
Neighborhood environment	
Use of neighborhood facilities index (Index 1)[b]	.12
Satisfaction with housing[c]	.38
Satisfaction with public services[d]	.09
Social fabric	
Neighboring index[e]	.16
Relatives living in the neighborhood (yes = 1; no = 0)	.11
Number of good friends living in neighborhood	−.01
Place of residence of primary social friend[f]	.07
Place of residence of primary provider of emotional supports[g]	.09
Belonging to neighborhood organizations[h]	.02
Respondent characteristics	
Number of children in household	.18
Age of respondent	.66
Household income	−.02
Nominal variable for race (black = 1; white = 0)	.07
Nominal variable for homeownership (homeowner = 1; renter = 0)	.51
Length of residence in neighborhood	−.06

[a]The classification function is derived in terms of those who are planning to stay in the neighborhood. Therefore, the higher a respondent's score, the greater the probability of that person's being classified as planning to stay in the neighborhood. The canonical correlation is 0.52; 77% of the cases were classified correctly; $N = 3,355$.
[b]Higher values connote greater use of neighborhood facilities.
[c]The survey question was scored 1 (very dissatisfied) to 5 (very satisfied); higher values show greater satisfaction.
[d]The survey question was scored 1 (very dissatisfied) to 5 (very satisfied); higher values show greater satisfaction.
[e]Higher values show increased neighboring.
[f]The survey question was scored 1 (outside of Pennsylvania) to 5 (in or near your neighborhood); higher values show closer proximity to the respondent.
[g]See note above for coding.
[h]The index was scored 0 (none) to 2 (belonging to at least two organizations located in or near the neighborhood); higher values show greater involvement.

Social fabric variables are not the most important discriminating variables; nonetheless, once other characteristics of the household are controlled for, social fabric is shown to have a positive effect on keeping people in the neighborhood.

CONCLUSION

This chapter stresses the importance of peoples' ties to their neighborhoods. Having been born there and having close personal connections to it are given by a large percentage of the respondents as the major reasons for moving into the neighborhood; the people living there is the second most important reason given for what the respondents like best about the neighborhood; and neighboring is an important discriminating variable for people who do not plan to move from the neighborhood.

The attachment of residents to their neighborhood and their satisfaction with it as a place to live were shown to be related to the personal ties that they had to the neighborhood and to their perceptions of the people living there. Respondents who were born in or moved into the neighborhood because of personal ties, respondents who mentioned the people living there as what they liked best about it, and respondents who did not see their neighbors as undesirable people were generally loyal, more attached, and more satisfied with the neighborhood than were others who did not express these sentiments.

The social fabric of the neighborhood is therefore important. It acts as a strong force to pull residents into the neighborhood and provides a strong incentive to hold them there. However, it does not affect all groups of people similarly. Catholics are drawn to their neighborhood because of intimate personal ties to a much greater extent than other religious groups, and blacks are motivated to a greater extent by reasons related to the affordability of housing and the quality of the environment.

The reasons for these differences are historical. Catholic neighborhoods have shown less turnover, in part because of the strength of the church. Blacks have experienced the effects of housing market discrimination which, until the last decade, has restricted their mobility. In addition, blacks have also been forced to move by factors over which they have had little control. Urban renewal in Pittsburgh destroyed several black neighborhoods and necessitated the movement of thousands of black households. This disruption necessarily destroyed the social cohesion of these neighborhoods and made it difficult for their social networks to be resurrected in new locations.

CHAPTER 5

The Impact of Neighborhood Support Systems on the Individual

INTRODUCTION

The previous chapter showed that the social fabric of the neighborhood is an important determinant of how people feel about their neighborhood. This chapter takes the analysis one step further and examines the relationship between various attributes of the neighborhood—particularly its social fabric and the support that it provides to the residents—and people's reported health, happiness, and life satisfaction. The framework used for the analysis is similar to that presented in previous chapters, and it draws upon the choice-constraint model. A person's physical and emotional health is assumed to be influenced by the characteristics of the individual, the neighborhood environment, and the social support system. Of particular interest here is the relationship between neighborhood sources of support and the health-related variables. Social supports are defined for this analysis to include those individuals to whom a person can turn for interpersonal aid or assistance, as well as neighborhood institutions which do or at least could provide a variety of services.[1]

[1]In James House's review of the social support literature, he indicated that

The literature generally differentiates between personal or social support systems and community support systems. Personal or social support systems consist of friends, family, neighbors, and colleagues who provide support, help, and personal care or concern for individuals. Community support systems consist of the supports or services provided within a community or neighborhood for helping residents meet their own social and emotional needs, as well as general welfare concerns. Community support systems therefore consist of resources within any given geographic area which can be potentially tapped by individuals in meeting their needs.[2] They also consist of informal networks of service care providers who deal with such specific problems as child care services,[3] the loss of a spouse,[4] marital and familial networks,[5] and even how information is gathered and shared.[6] The research described in this chapter focuses primarily upon the personal support system. The community support system is partially accounted for by considering the presence of institutions in the neighborhood for shopping, worship, recreation, and health services and by membership in voluntary organizations.

---

there is little general agreement on the definition of social support, beyond the fact that the notion of social support connotes positive, constructive interpersonal aid or assistance. See James S. House, *Work Stress and Social Support* (Reading, Ma.: Addison-Wesley, 1980).

[2]Gerald Caplan, *Support Systems and Community Mental Health* (New York: Behavioral Publications, 1974); and David Biegel and Arthur Naparstek, ed. *Community Support Systems and Mental Health* (New York: Springer Publishing Company, 1982).

[3]Alice H. Collins and Diane L. Pancoast, *Natural Helping Networks* (Washington, D.C.: National Association of Social Workers, 1976).

[4]Phyllis R. Silverman, "The Widow to Widow Program: An Experiment in Preventive Intervention," *Mental Hygiene 53* (1969): 333–37.

[5]Elizabeth Bott, *Family and Social Networks,* 2nd ed. (London: Tavistock Publications, 1971).

[6]James Allen Barnes, "Networks and Political Process," in *Social Networks In Urban Situations,* ed. J. C. Mitchell (Manchester, England: University of Manchester Press, 1969).

There is agreement in the literature that the members of an individual's social support system help in some way, particularly as buffers or protectors against stress.[7] Individuals who are positively linked to a support system of friends or relatives appear to have a number of advantages in terms of their quality of life and level of both mental and physical health, but there is still a great deal which is not known about the specific ways in which the support systems of individuals function and how helpful or effective such systems are from the perspective of the central figure.

In recent years there has been a growing interest in or reemphasis upon using family, friends, neighbors, work colleagues, and a wide variety of resource people within communities and neighborhoods to help individuals cope with the problems and stresses of modern day life.[8] These various resource people provide emotional support as well as other substantive resources and may serve as buffers and even therapists for those in need. The beneficial results of this social support system are pervasive. Epidemiological research shows that there are certain populations which are at risk primarily because they have no social supports among their own friends or within their own community.[9]

[7]For a discussion, see Aaron Antonovsky, *Health, Stress and Coping* (San Francisco: Jossey-Bass Publishers, 1979); John Cassel, "The Contribution of the Social Environment Host Resistance," *American Journal of Epidemiology* 102(2) (1976): 107–23; Alfred Dean and Nan Lin, "The Stress-Buffering Role of Social Support: Problems and Prospects for Systematic Investigation," *Journal of Nervous and Mental Disease* 165(6) (1977): 403–17; William W. Eaton, "Life Events, Social Supports and Psychiatric Symptoms: A Reanalysis of the New Haven Data," *Journal of Health and Social Behavior* 19 (1978): 230–34; and Hans Selye, "Forty Years of Stress Research: Principal Remaining Problems and Misconceptions," *CMA Journal* 115 (1976): 53–6.

[8]President's Commission on Mental Health, *Final Report Vol. II, Task Panel Reports* (Washington, D.C.: U.S. Government Printing Office, 1978).

[9]See Cassel, "Contribution of the Social Environment Host Resistance"; Dean and Lin, "Stress-Buffering Role of Social Support"; Eaton, "Life

There is also research by Fischer and others[10] which indicates that those same populations are also at a disadvantage in terms of their support systems and networks of friends, relatives, and colleagues. The President's Task Panel Report,[11] as well as the Collins and Pancoast[12] work on natural helping networks, shows that there is a long history of the involvement of natural helping networks and support systems in health and mental health.

Much of the recent research interest in social support systems has been motivated by research dealing with the psychological as well as the physical effects of stress. The interaction of social supports and life stresses is not totally understood, but it has been investigated by a number of researchers. In one study by Nuckolls, Cassel, and Kaplan the interactive effects of stress and social support were clearly evident.[13] The investigators surmised that women with high assets or social supports are less susceptible to a variety of "environmental insults," but they are careful to point out that several diverse factors must be considered. Another study by Gore took a longitudinal approach to assess the differential impact of unemployment upon men with varying levels of support.[14] She found that those with social supports had fewer health problems and lower levels

---

Events, Social Supports and Psychiatric Symptoms"; and Susan Gore, "The Effects of Social Support in Moderating the Health Consequences of Unemployment," *Journal of Health and Social Behavior 19* (1978): 157–65.

[10]Claude S. Fischer, Robert M. Jackson, C. Ann Stueve, Kathleen Gerson, and Lynne McCallister-Jones, with Mark Baldassare, *Networks and Places: Social Relations in the Urban Setting* (New York: The Free Press, 1977).

[11]President's Commission on Mental Health, *Final Report vol. 2.*

[12]Collins and Pancoast, *Natural Helping Networks.*

[13]Katherine B. Nuckolls, John Cassel, and Bertram H. Kaplan, "Psychosocial Assets, Life Crisis and the Prognosis of Pregnancy," *American Journal of Epidemiology 95* (1972): 431–41.

[14]Gore, "Effects of Social Support in Moderating the Health Consequences of Unemployment."

of life stress. A study by Lin and colleagues looks more specifically at stressful life events and social supports and concludes that stresses are positively related to symptoms, and social supports are negatively related to symptoms, and therefore social support acts as a mediator between stress and illness.[15] Cassel draws a similar conclusion in his review of a variety of related studies.[16]

The literature shows that there is clearly a direct relationship between social support and stress. The relationship between social supports and health is not so well established. It could be direct with stronger social supports being directly associated with fewer health problems; it could be indirect with stronger social supports being associated with reduced life stress and the lower levels of stress being associated with better physical health; or it could be both.[17]

THE MODEL

The model which serves as the framework for the analysis described in this chapter is shown in Figure 2. It spec-

[15]Nan Lin, Walter M. Ensel, Ronald S. Simeone, and Wen Kuo, "Social Support, Stressful Life Events and Illness: A Model and an Empirical Test," *Journal of Health and Social Behavior 29* (1979): 108–19.

[16]Cassel, "Contribution of the Social Environment Host Resistance."

[17]A discussion of this point is contained in Gerald Caplan and Marie Killilea, *Support Systems and Mutual Help* (New York: Grune & Stratton, 1976); R. D. Caplan *et al.*, *Adhering to Medical Regimes: Pilot Experiments in Patient Education and Social Support* (Ann Arbor: Institute for Social Research, 1976); Cassel, "Contribution of the Social Environment Host Resistance"; Sidney Cobb, "Social Support and Health through the Life Cycle," paper presented at the annual meeting of the American Association for the Advancement of Science, 1978; Sidney Cobb, "Social Support as a Moderator of Life Stress," *Psychosomatic Medicine 38*(5) (1976): 300–14; A. R. Kagan and L. Levi, "Health and Environment— Psychosocial Stimuli: A Review," *Social Science and Medicine 8* (1974): 225–41; and Bertram H. Kaplan, John C. Cassel and Susan Gore, "Social Support and Health," *Medical Care 25* (Supplement 1977): 47–58.

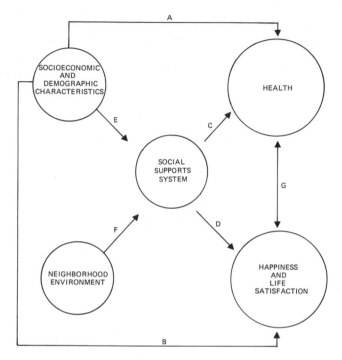

Figure 2. Model of variables influencing an individual's health and mental health.

ifies that certain aspects of a person's health and attitudes about life are influenced by socioeconomic characteristics of the respondent (links A and B) and by the characteristics of the social supports system (links C and D), including whether or not it is based in the wider community. The characteristics of the social support system, as shown in previous chapters, are in turn influenced by some of the socioeconomic and demographic characteristics of the respondent (link E) and by some of the characteristics of the neighborhood environment (link F). There is also a direct relationship between happiness and life satisfaction and health (link G).

The direction of the relationship between social supports and health and between social supports and happiness/satisfaction is shown in the model to run from social supports to the health and happiness/satisfaction variables. The cause-and-effect relationship could be argued to run in the opposite direction, but some of the literature provides evidence to show that social supports determine health and mental health (happiness and life satisfaction may be thought of as proxies for certain aspects of an individual's mental health) and not vice versa.[18] The current research, being cross-sectional in nature, will not permit a more definitive conclusion. It shows only that there is or is not a statistically significant relationship between certain variables. These relationships are examined through the use of multiple regression analysis, and the variables included in the equations are discussed in the next section.

DESCRIPTION OF THE VARIABLES

Happiness and Life Satisfaction

The following two survey questions were used as proxies for the respondents' overall mental health:

1. Taking all things together, how would you say things are these days—would you say you are very happy, pretty happy, or not too happy? (The question is adapted from the work of Bradburn; Campbell, Converse, & Rodgers; and Gurin, Veroff, & Feld.[19])

---

[18]For instance, see Lisa F. Berkman and S. Leonard Syme, "Social Networks, Host Resistance and Mortality: A Nine-Year Follow-Up Study of Alameda County Residents," *American Journal of Epidemiology* 109(2) (1979): 186–204; Nuckolls, Cassel, and Kaplan, "Psychosocial Assets, Life Crisis and the Prognosis of Pregnancy"; and Beverley Raphael, "Preventive Intervention with the Recently Bereaved," *Archives of General Psychiatry* 34 (1977): 1450–54.

[19]Norman M. Bradburn, *The Structure of Psychological Well-Being* (Chicago: Aldine, 1969); Angus Campbell, Philip E. Converse, and Willard L. Rodgers, *The Quality of American Life: Perceptions, Evaluations and Satisfactions* (New York: Russell Sage Foundation, 1976); and Gerald Gurin, Joseph Veroff, and Sheila Feld, *Americans View Their Mental Health* (New York: Basic Books, 1960).

2. Now I would like to ask you about your life as a whole. In general, are you very satisfied, satisfied, neither satisfied nor dissatisfied, dissatisfied, or very dissatisfied with your life as a whole these days? (Adapted from Campbell, Converse, & Rodgers.[20])

Health

The following question was used to capture the respondents' overall health status: "How has your health been over the last year or so? Would you say you have been in poor health, fair health, good health, or excellent health?"

Socioeconomic and Demographic Characteristics

Variables used to describe socioeconomic and demographic characteristics included:

- Age
- Household income
- Race (black or white)
- Length of time in neighborhood (this variable was eventually dropped from the analysis because it was never statistically significant)
- Number of children under 18 living in the household
- Marital status
- Work status
- Sex

In addition to the above variables, the extent of the respondent's participation in voluntary organizations was included in the analysis. Participation provides the respondent with another avenue to communicate with others and to form interpersonal relationships, and therefore it was

---

[20]Campbell, Converse, and Rodgers, *The Quality of American Life: Perceptions, Evaluations and Satisfactions,* 1976.

felt that it may be a factor contributing to the respondent's health and perceptions of life. A participation index was created which added together the respondent's responses to each of the following two questions:

- Participation in a neighborhood organization (yes; no)
- Participation in other voluntary organizations (yes; no)

Social Support System

Social support has been measured in a variety of ways in the literature. Specifically, Nuckolls, Cassel, and Kaplan used an instrument which they developed to measure what they called "psychosocial assets."[21] This instrument examined the number of close friends and relatives a person had, as well as the frequency and type of contact. Gore operationally defined social support in her study of unemployed men by using an index which included the individual's perception of the supportiveness of spouse, relatives, and friends and the frequency with which the relationship was satisfying or provided an opportunity to discuss a problem.[22] Lin *et al.* assessed social support using a nine-item scale of the individual's involvement and interaction with friends, neighbors, cultural and community activities, and other non-kin support.[23] Cassel assessed social support from a more sociological perspective in that he views "marginal" people (for example, those who have undergone frequent occupational transitions) as being more susceptible to disease.[24]

---

[21]Nuckolls, Cassel, and Kaplan, "Psychosocial Assets, Life Crisis and the Prognosis of Pregnancy."

[22]Gore, "Effects of Social Support in Moderating the Health Consequences of Unemployment."

[23]Lin, Ensel, Simeone, and Kuo, "Social Support, Stressful Life Events and Illness."

[24]Cassel, "Contribution of the Social Environment Host Resistance."

The investigation of support systems has also been approached by some researchers through the use of social network analysis.[25] Through this approach a number of descriptive variables have been developed to assess in more precise terms the quantitative and qualitative aspects of the relationships which people have with each other. Variables that have been operationalized by network analysts include the following: multiplexity (the number of ways in which a person knows another person—as a relative and a neighbor and a member of a community organization, and so forth; and the content of the interaction); symmetry (balance between the supports provided by A to B, and those provided by B to A); intensity of the relationship; range (the number of providers of support); density (the interlinkage among the number of providers of support within a person's support system); and clustering (the extent to which the support system is divided into distinguishable cliques).

The analysis of the social support system in this research was based upon a number of the dimensions identified by the network analysts. The social support system was operationalized for analytical purposes through the following survey responses:

- Number of people the respondent considers to be really good friends
- Frequency of contact with the person with whom the respondent discusses personal concerns
- Extent to which the individuals identified as part of the respondent's social support network know each other (density)

[25]For example, see James Allen Barnes, *Social Networks,* Addison-Wesley Module in Anthropology No. 26, 1972; Bott, *Family and Social Networks;* Fischer *et al., Networks and Places;* and J. C. Mitchell, *Social Networks in Urban Situations.*

Neighborhood Attributes

Specific aspects of the neighborhood which may contribute to the formulation or strengthening of support systems were examined. These include:

- Whether or not the respondent has relatives living in the neighborhood.
- Neighboring activity. A neighboring index was constructed by summing and weighting equally the respondents' answers to the following four questions: Frequency of borrowing or exchanging things with neighbors, frequency of visiting neighbors, frequency of helping (or being helped by) neighbors with small tasks, and willingness to call on neighbors for help in an emergency.
- Use of neighborhood facilities. A neighborhood facilities use index was constructed by summing and weighting equally answers to the survey questions which asked the respondents how often they did the following in or near their neighborhood: main grocery shopping, shopping for small items, attending church or other religious organizations, used health or medical services and engaged in recreation activities.

Satisfaction with Housing and Neighborhood

In order to capture other dimensions of the respondents' living environment which may influence their outlook on life and affect their health/mental health, the following general attitudes of the respondents were included in the analysis:

- Satisfaction with home or apartment
- Satisfaction with the neighborhood

RESULTS

The research, using the basic framework shown in Figure 2, attempted to identify the independent variables which are the most important explanatory variables for differences in the health, happiness, and life satisfaction of the respondents. Three models were used for analytical purposes (see Equations 1, 2, and 3). The first model (Equation 1) included independent variables which account for differences in socioeconomic characteristics of the respondents, their social support systems, their health or mental health, depending upon which equation was being estimated, and certain attributes of the neighborhood. Equation 2 added a variable which captures the respondents' satisfaction with their housing. Equation 3 added another variable which attempts to hold constant the respondents' satisfaction with their neighborhood. These additional variables were included in the analysis because it is reasonable to expect that people's feelings about their housing and their neighborhood will affect how they feel about their health and life in general. It is encouraging to see that most of the statistically significant independent variables remain no matter which model is used and that the conclusions of the research do not depend upon the way in which the model is specified.

The results of the analysis are shown in Tables 14, 15, and 16. Each of the independent variables is discussed in the balance of this section.

(1) $\quad MH = a_0 + a_1C + a_2SS + a_3H + a_4NA$

(1a) $\quad H = b_0 + b_1C + b_2SS + b_3MH + b_4NA$

(2) $\quad MH = c_0 + c_1C + c_2SS + c_3H + c_4NA + c_5SH$

(2a) $\quad H = d_0 + d_1C + d_2SS + d_3MH + d_4NA + d_5SH$

(3) $\quad MH = e_0 + e_1C + e_2SS + e_3H + e_4NA + e_5HS + e_6SN$

(3a) $\quad H = f_0 + f_1C + f_2SS + f_3MH + f_4NA + f_5SH + f_6SN$

where *MH* = happiness and life satisfaction, *H* = health proxy, a_0-f_0 = constant terms, $a_{1-4}-f_{1-6}$ = coefficients, *C* = socioeconomic and demographic characteristics, *SS* = structure of the social supports system, *NA* = certain attributes of the neighborhood, *SH* = satisfaction with housing, and *SN* = satisfaction with the neighborhood environment.

Table 14. Multiple Regression Analysis: Life Happiness[a]

Independent variables[b]	Beta coefficients		
	Run #1	Run #2	Run #3
Relatives in neighborhood (N = 0; Y = 1)	−.04*	−.04*	−.04*
Number of close friends	.08*	.07*	.07*
Frequency of contact	.03	.02	.02
Network density	—	—	—
Neighboring index	.10*	.08*	.04*
Neighborhood facilities index	.09*	.08*	.04*
Participation in voluntary organizations (N = 0; Y = 1)	.04*	.04*	.03
Age of respondent	.02	−.01	−.04*
Household income	.08*	.05*	.01
Number of children in household	−.08*	−.06*	−.06*
Marital status (M = 0; Other = 1)	−.05*	−.04*	−.04*
Work status (EmpFT = 0; Other = 1)	.03	.02	.02
Sex (M = 0; F = 1)	.05*	.05*	.04*
Race (W = 0; B = 1)	−.04*	−.01	.02
Health	.17*	.15*	.14*
Satisfaction with home/apartment	x	.20*	.14*
Satisfaction with neighborhood	x	x	.28*
R^2	.10	.13	.20
N	5,365	5,365	5,365

[a]Dependent variable: taking all things together, how would you say things are these days—would you say you are very happy, pretty happy, or not too happy?
[b]A description of these variables is contained in Table 17.
* = Statistically significant at $p = 0.05$.
x = Variable not included in the equation.
— = Coefficient less than 0.01.

Table 15. Multiple Regression Analysis: Life Satisfaction[a]

Independent variables[b]	Beta coefficients		
	Run #1	Run #2	Run #3
Relatives in neighborhood (N = 0; Y = 1)	−.03*	−.03*	−.03*
Number of close friends	.10*	.09*	.09*
Frequency of contact	.04*	.03*	.03*
Network density	.02	.02	.02
Neighboring index	.06*	.04*	.03*
Neighborhood facilities index	.07*	.05*	.04*
Participation in voluntary organizations (N = 0; Y = 1)	.03*	.03*	.03*
Age of respondent	.08*	.04*	.03*
Household income	.08*	.05*	.04*
Number of children in household	−.07*	−.05*	−.05*
Marital status (M = 0; Other = 1)	−.10*	−.10*	−.10*
Work status (EmpFT = 0; Other = 1)	.01	.01	.01
Sex (M = 0; F = 1)	.05*	.05*	.04*
Race (W = 0; B = 1)	−.03*	—	.01
Health	.25*	.23*	.22*
Satisfaction with home/ apartment	x	.20*	.18*
Satisfaction with neighborhood	x	x	.10*
R^2	.13	.17	.17
N	5,365	5,365	5,365

[a]Dependent variable: in general, are you very satisfied, satisfied, neither satisfied nor dissatisfied, dissatisfied, or very dissatisfied with your life as a whole these days?
[b]A description of these variables is contained in Table 17.
  * = Statistically significant at $p = 0.05$.
  x = Variable not included in the equation.
  — = Coefficient less than 0.01.

Relatives in the Neighborhood. Surprisingly, respondents with relatives living in the neighborhood are less happy, and less satisfied and report poorer health than do respondents having no relatives in the neighborhood. This could reflect the fact that people with a higher incidence of health and mental health problems move closer to their

Table 16. Multiple Regression Analysis: Health Status[a]

Independent variables[b]	Beta coefficients		
	Run #1	Run #2	Run #3
Relatives in neighborhood (N = 0; Y = 1)	−.03*	−.03*	−.03*
Number of close friends	.02	.02	.02
Frequency of contact	−.02	−.02	−.02
Network density	−.02*	−.02*	−.02*
Neighboring index	−.01	−.02	−.02
Neighborhood facilities index	.02	.02	.02
Participation in voluntary organizations (N = 0; Y = 1)	.03*	.03*	.03*
Age of respondent	−.31*	−.31*	−.31*
Household income	.14*	.13*	.13*
Number of children in household	—	—	—
Marital status (M = 0; Other = 1)	.04*	.04*	.04*
Work status (EmpFT = 0; Other = 1)	−.08*	−.08*	−.08*
Sex (M = 0; F = 1)	−.04*	−.04*	−.04*
Race (W = 0; B = 1)	−.06*	−.06*	−.05*
Happiness	.08*	.08*	.07*
Life satisfaction	.19*	.18*	.18*
Satisfaction with home/ apartment	x	.03*	.03*
Satisfaction with neighborhood	x	x	.01
R^2	.26	.26	.26
N	5,365	5,365	5,365

[a]Dependent variable: how has your health been over the last year or so? would you say you have been in poor health, fair health, or excellent health?
[b]A description of these variables is contained in Table 17.
  * = Statistically significant at $p = 0.05$.
  x = Variable not included in the equation.
  — = Coefficient less than 0.01.

relatives or that their relatives move closer to them. The analysis cannot directly explain this result; however, the data show that respondents who have relatives in the neighborhood have lived there for longer periods of time than those who do not and that those having relatives in the neighborhood are generally older; therefore this variable may be capturing some of the effects of the age variable.

Number of Close Friends. The more close friends a respondent has, the greater that person's happiness and life satisfaction. The variable is not statistically significant in the health equations.

Frequency of Contact with the Provider of Emotional Supports. This variable was not statistically significant in the happiness and health equations, but it was for all three of the life satisfaction equations. (A variation of this variable was also used in the regression equations—the place of residence of the provider of emotional supports with higher values showing a location closer to that of the respondent—but this variable was not statistically significant and it was dropped from the analysis.)

Network Density. Network density was not statistically significant in the happiness or life satisfaction equation, but it was significant and inversely related to health. This may occur as a result of deteriorating health—as a person's health problems increase, there is greater need for others to provide care, and as they do so, they meet other members of the individual's support network.

Neighboring Index. Those who neighbor more are happier and more satisfied. This makes sense. Increased interpersonal contact provides people with greater opportunity to discuss events and problems which may create stress if not resolved or at least brought out into the open. The neighboring index is not statistically significant in the health question.

Use of Neighborhood Facilities. Respondents who made greater use of the neighborhood (shopping, worship, and recreation) were happier and more satisfied. This may occur because these people have greater opportunity to interact with their neighbors and therefore have a larger pool of potential people with whom they can talk over stressful situations. This index was not statistically significant in the health equations.

Participation in Voluntary Organizations. People who participate are happier and more satisfied and have fewer reported health problems than those who do not. This could mean either that participation by itself has positive health and mental health effects or that those who have fewer health and mental health problems are the people most likely to participate.

Age. Age is statistically significant in the life happiness analysis when all other variables are held constant, and it is negatively related to happiness. Age is positively related to life satisfaction in all three equations; and in the health analysis it is the dominant explanatory variable and is inversely related to the dependent variable.

Income. Income is directly related to all three independent variables in all cases except when neighborhood satisfaction is controlled for in the happiness regression analysis. In this case, the neighborhood satisfaction variable probably captured some of the effects of income. The direct relationship between income and the dependent variables is not too surprising. People with more resources have greater access to health care and have greater opportunities to avail themselves of a myriad of different services than do those who are financially deprived.

Number of Children Less Than 18 Years of Age Living in the Household. Households with a greater number of children are less happy and are less satisfied than those with fewer children. This variable is not statistically significant in the health equation.

Marital Status. People who are married are happier and more satisfied with life than those who are not married. However, married respondents report lower health status than do others.

Work Status. An individual's work status does not affect attitudes about life; however, those who are employed report fewer health problems than those who are not. There is nothing surprising in this result. People who have significant health problems would normally not be expected to be working at a full-time job.

Sex. Women are happier and more satisfied than men but report more health problems than men.

Race. In the models in which race is statistically significant, blacks are less happy and less satisfied and report poorer health than do whites. This result is not too surprising. Blacks are more constrained to place than whites and therefore have less opportunity to avail themselves of needed services or to form satisfying relationships.

Health. This is the most important explanatory variable for life satisfaction and second most important for happiness.

Happiness and Life Satisfaction. Both are statistically significant in the health equation, and life satisfaction is the second most important explantory variable.

Satisfaction with Home/Apartment. Satisfaction with one's home or apartment is the second most important explanatory variable in the third life satisfaction equation and tied for second most important explanatory variable in the third equation of the happiness analysis. It is also statistically significant in the health analysis. In all cases, this variable relates positively to the dependent variable. It is not possible to infer a cause-and-effect relationship between this independent variable and any of the three dependent variables. Greater satisfaction with one's dwelling unit could lead to less life stress and fewer mental health problems, or better health and more positive feelings about life could lead to higher levels of satisfaction with other aspects of one's life.

Table 17. Description of the Variables Used in the Multiple Regression Equations

---

1. *Relatives in the neighborhood.* Coded Yes = 1; No = 0
2. *Number of close friends.* Actual number reported.
3. *Frequency of contact.* The respondent's frequency of contact with his or her provider of emotional supports was measured on a 6-point scale, with higher values corresponding to more frequent contact.
4. *Network density.* This variable measures the degree to which the individuals mentioned in the respondents' social and emotional support network know one another; higher values show that a greater percentage of the individuals identified in the network know each other.
5. *Neighboring index.* Constructed by summing and weighting equally answers to the following four survey questions: Frequency of bor-

---

(continued)

Table 17. (continued)

rowing or exchanging things with neighbors; frequency of visiting neighbors; frequency of helping (or being helped by) neighbors with small tasks; and willingness to call on neighbors for help in an emergency. The borrowing, visiting, and helping questions were coded on a 4-point scale, with higher values showing more frequent neighboring; the emergency question was coded Yes = 1; No = 0.

6. *Neighborhood facilities index.* Constructed by summing and weighting equally answers to the survey questions which asked the respondents how often they did the following in or near their neighborhood: main grocery shopping; shopping for small items; attending church or other religious organizations; use of health facilities or medical services; and engaged in recreation activities. The questions were coded on a 4-point scale, with higher values showing more frequent use in or near the neighborhood.

7. *Participation in voluntary organizations.* Respondents were asked whether they participated in an organization concerned with neighborhood issues (coded Yes = 1; No = 0) and whether they participated in other voluntary organizations such as a church group, PTA, recreation, fraternal, civic, etc. (coded Yes = 1; No = 0). The respondents' answers to the two questions were added together to create a participation index. Higher values show greater participation.

8. *Age of respondent.* Actual age.

9. *Household income.* Actual reported income.

10. *Number of children in household.* Actual number of children under 18 years of age.

11. *Marital status.* Coded married = 0; any other status = 1.

12. *Work status.* Coded employed full time = 0; any other status (including not participating in the labor market) = 1.

13. *Sex.* Coded females = 1; males = 0.

14. *Race.* Coded black = 1; white = 0.

15. *Health.* Respondents were asked to rate their health over the past year. Responses were coded on a 4-point scale with higher values showing better health.

16. *Happiness.* Respondents were asked about their happiness. Responses were coded on a 4-point scale, with higher values showing greater life happiness.

17. *Life satisfaction.* Respondents were asked about their satisfaction with life as a whole. Responses were measured on a 5-point scale, with higher values corresponding to greater satisfaction.

18. *Satisfaction with home/apartment.* Measured on a 5-point scale with higher values showing increased satisfaction.

19. *Satisfaction with neighborhood.* Respondents were asked to rate the neighborhood as a place to live. Responses were measured on a 4-point scale with higher values corresponding to greater satisfaction.

Satisfaction with the Neighborhood. Satisfaction with the neighborhood is the most important explanatory variable in the happiness analysis and tied for the third most important in the life satisfaction analysis. It is not statistically significant in the health equation. As with satisfaction with home or apartment, it is not possible to discern the causal direction between this variable and the dependent variables.

DISCUSSION

The analysis shows that an individual's social support system makes a positive contribution to happiness and life satisfaction. Respondents with more close friends, those who neighbor more frequently, and those who are married are happier and more satisfied. Frequency of contact with the person who provides emotional supports is also directly related to life satisfaction but not to happiness. Surprisingly, having relatives in the neighborhood is negatively related to the dependent variable in the equation when it is statistically significant. Network density was found not to be a statistically significant explanatory variable.

The analysis also shows that those who use the neighborhood for shopping, worship, recreation, and other activities and those who participate in voluntary organizations have higher levels of happiness and life satisfaction than those who do not. This, coupled with the positive relationship between neighboring and the happiness and life satisfaction variables, suggests that the neighborhood makes an important contribution to the feelings that people have about their life.

There does not appear to be a strong relationship between a person's social support system and health. The only variables that are statistically significant are relatives in the neighborhood and network density, and these are negatively related to health.

The relationship between health and people's attitudes

about life is confirmed by the analysis. Happiness and life satisfaction are statistically significant in the health equations, and the health variable is statistically significant in the mental health equations.

The significance of the conclusions in this chapter must be put in the context of the explanatory power of the regression equations. There is a large amount of unexplained variance in the equations, and this could be a result of the specification of the equations, the particular variables used in the analysis, and/or the quality of the data. The general, and self-reported, nature of the dependent variables could have introduced a large amount of variance which could not be accounted for by the specific independent variables used. The three variables used as dependent variables are broad attitudinal indicators, and they most likely capture a variety of dimensions of the respondents' lives. To the extent that happiness (or life satisfaction) means a number of different things to different people (and these subdimensions vary across the population surveyed), the low explanatory power of the equations is not surprising. An attempt was made in the analysis to control for some of these variations with the inclusion of the satisfaction variables for home or apartment and neighborhood, but this did not significantly raise the explanatory power of the equations.

The low explanatory power may also arise because of limitations in the availability of data to describe the support system. For instance, data were not available to assess the quality of the support system. Finally, the low explanatory power may not be terribly surprising in light of the fact that the population surveyed was a normal one and the survey did not focus specifically on those with health and mental health problems.

The analysis shows that those who have the greatest economic resources are happier, more satisfied, and in better health. This may result not only from their having a greater financial ability to take care of problems as they arise, but also from the fact that these individuals have greater access to people and hence have a larger population pool from which to select their friends and confidants. This may increase their ability to form a social support system which best meets their needs.

Likewise, the populations most at risk are those with the fewest resources. Lower-income, elderly respondents reported the greatest health problems and lowest levels of life happiness. If these individuals happen to live in neighborhoods in which supportive institutions are lacking, the life stresses they confront on a day-to-day basis may be difficult for them to ameliorate without some other forms of outside assistance.

While showing that certain aspects of the neighborhood are statistically significant, the analysis shows that it is the presence or absence of a support system which is important and not necessarily the location of the persons involved. This is consistent with the community of limited liability. This concept implies a somewhat superficial set of neighborhood relationships—that is, the neighborhood does not penetrate too deeply into the lives of the residents. Individuals who are able to do so can reach outside of their neighborhood for the help they require or the meaningful relationships they need if they so desire. Thus their opportunity set is expanded. Those who are more constrained to place will have fewer opportunities to meet their needs; therefore it is not surprising that these individuals are less happy and less satisfied and report more health problems.

This chapter, like the previous ones, illustrates the importance of certain aspects of the neighborhood environment. People's feelings about their place of residence and their happiness and general life satisfaction are associated with neighboring and the use of neighborhood-based institutions. Therefore, the neighborhood plays an important role in the lives of many of its residents, and it is particularly important for those having the least opportunity to participate outside of the neighborhood.

CHAPTER 6

Neighborhood Social Fabric

INTRODUCTION

Previous chapters have shown that different groups of people create their own social fabric and that actions and attitudes become a part of it. The structure of the social fabric of a neighborhood is therefore a useful starting point for understanding the less visible strengths and weaknesses of that area as a residential community. Social fabric in previous chapters has been discussed in broad terms to include dimensions of interpersonal relationships, participation in neighborhood organizations, and the uses made of neighborhood-based institutions. All of these factors were assumed to work together to create the intangible substance labeled *social fabric.* However, the discussion in the earlier chapters showed that the strength of different elements of the social fabric varied depending upon the characteristics of the residents. For instance, higher-income residents—those with the greatest potential economic mobility—neighbor more frequently and participate in neighborhood organizations at higher rates than the rest of the population. These individuals also have the most extensive ties outside of the neighborhood in terms of their social and emotional support systems. Consequently, it is reasonable to assume that the strength of the distinct dimensions of social fabric will vary among neighborhoods which have different economic and institutional characteristics.

One would also expect that as the important social and emotional dimensions of peoples' lives shift from the locus of neighborhood to the greater community, their allegiance, commitment, and attachment to the neighborhood should change. This implies that the social fabric of the neighborhood may be weaker, or at least different, in neighborhoods in which residents have stronger external ties than it is in neighborhoods with relatively stronger internal ties. This chapter examines these relationships in detail.

INTERNAL AND EXTERNAL TIES

The following information was gathered in the survey in order to try to assess the composition of the various elements comprising the social fabric of each of Pittsburgh's 74 neighborhoods. To the extent that these activities occur or relationships exist more frequently in or near the neighborhood, the social fabric was considered to be stronger than if they were located outside of the neighborhood.

Personal ties to neighborhood:
- Percentage of residents with relatives living in their neighborhood
- Percentage of residents with best social friend living in their neighborhood
- Percentage of residents with the person they depend upon to discuss their personal concerns living in their neighborhood
- Average number of good friends living in the neighborhood

Neighboring:
- Percentage of residents likely to borrow or exchange things with their neighbors
- Percentage of residents likely to visit with their neighbors
- Percentage of residents likely to help or be

helped by their neighbors with small tasks such as repair work or grocery shopping
- Percentage of residents willing to call on neighbors for help in an emergency

Participation in neighborhood organizations:
- Percentage of residents belonging to an organization which is concerned about issues or problems in their neighborhood
- Percentage of residents belonging to other organizations such as church groups, PTAs, fraternal, civic, and so on in their neighborhood

Use of neighborhood institutions:
- Percentage of residents doing their main grocery shopping in their neighborhood
- Percentage of residents shopping for small items in their neighborhood
- Percentage of residents attending church or synagogue in their neighborhood

Place of work:
- Percentage of residents working in their neighborhood

Relationships among the Variables

A matrix showing the correlations between the survey questions used to examine the presence of internal and external ties is shown in Table 18. The correlations, at the neighborhood level, are computed for all of Pittsburgh's 74 neighborhoods. The statistically significant relationships (correlation of approximately 0.20 and above) are discussed below for each of the survey questions.

Relatives Living in the Neighborhood. Neighborhoods with higher percentages of their residents having relatives in the neighborhood are also those with higher percentages of their residents' best social friend and provider of emotional supports residing in the neighborhood. These neigh-

Table 18. Correlation Matrix at Neighborhood Level: Internal and

	1. Shopping	2. Worship	3. Neighboring	4. Percentage with relatives in neighborhood	5. Percentage with best social friends	6. Percentage with provider of emotional support in neighborhood	7. Mean number of friends
1. Shopping	1.00	.32*	.23**	−.06	−.19	−.08	.16
2. Worship	.32*	1.00	.58*	.38*	.14	.21**	.45*
3. Neighboring	.23**	.58*	1.00	.13	—	.05	.31*
4. Percentage with relatives in neighborhood	−.06	.38*	.13	1.00	.55*	.67*	.46*
5. Percentage with primary social friend in neighborhood	−.19	.14	—	.55*	1.00	.61*	.32*
6. Percentage with provider of emotional support in neighborhood	−.08	.21**	.05	.67*	.61*	1.00	.38*
7. Mean number of friends in neighborhood	.16	.45*	.31*	.46*	.32*	.38*	1.00
8. Percentage belonging to neighborhood organization	−.03	−.16	.07	.12	.08	.05	—
9. Percentage belonging to voluntary organizations	.19	.18	.17	.27**	.16	.21**	.22**

8. Percentage belonging to neighborhood organization	9. Percentage belonging to voluntary organizations	10. Percentage who work in neighborhood	11. Mean income	12. Percentage of home-ownership	13. Percentage of blacks	14. Percentage of Catholics	15. Mean years living in neighborhood
−.03	.19	.41*	.26**	−.04	−.47*	.36*	−.04
−.16	.18	.05	.22**	.44*	−.59*	.79*	.50*
.07	.17	−.02	.58*	.51*	−.62*	.58*	.16
.12	.27**	.04	−.16	.34*	−.12	.39*	.79*
.08	.16	.20**	−.34*	−.02	.17	.09	.51*
.05	.21**	.16	−.14	.13	.07	.17	.51*
—	.22**	.19**	−.12	.26**	−.15	.39*	.50*
1.00	.28**	.08	.10	.20**	.12	−.25**	.08
.28*	1.00	.10	.17	.26**	−.08	.05	.25**

(continued)

Table 18. (continued)

	1. Shopping	2. Worship	3. Neighboring	4. Percentage with relatives in neighborhood	5. Percentage with best social friends	6. Percentage with provider of emotional support in neighborhood	7. Mean number of friends
10. Percentage who work in neighborhood	.41*	.05	−.02	.04	.20**	.16	.19**
11. Mean income	.26**	.22**	.58*	−.16	−.34*	−.14	−.12
12. Percentage of home-ownership	−.04	.44*	.51*	.34*	−.02	.13	.26**
13. Percentage of blacks	−.47*	−.59*	−.62*	−.12	.17	.07	−.15
14. Percentage of Catholics	.36*	.79*	.58*	.39*	.09	.17	.39*
15. Mean years living in neighborhood	−.04	.50*	.16	.79*	.51*	.51*	.50*

[a]Explanation:
1. Shopping. The index was constructed by adding the respondent's answer to the survey questions which asked (1) how often do you do your main grocery shopping in or near your neighborhood, and (2) how often do you use stores in your neighborhood for shopping for small items, dry cleaning, etc. The questions were coded on a 4-point scale (1 = none, 4 = all). Higher values of the index show increased neighborhood shopping.
2. Worship. Survey question: How often do you attend religious services in or near your neighborhood (coded as above). Higher values show greater frequency of worship in or near the neighborhood.
3. Neighboring. The index was constructed by summing and weighting equally answers to the following four survey questions: frequency of borrowing or exchanging things with neighbors; frequency of visiting neighbors; frequency of helping (or being helped by) neighbors with small tasks; and willingness to call on neighbors for help in an emergency. The borrowing, visiting, and helping questions were coded on a 4-point scale, with higher values showing more frequent neighboring; the emergency question was coded Yes = 1; No = 0. Higher values of the index show more frequent neighboring.
4. Percentage of respondents with relatives living in the neighborhood.

8. Percentage belonging to neighborhood organization	9. Percentage belonging to voluntary organizations	10. Percentage who work in neighborhood	11. Mean income	12. Percentage of home-ownership	13. Percentage of blacks	14. Percentage of Catholics	15. Mean years living in neighborhood
.08	.10	1.00	−.16	−.29**	−.20**	.12	.11
.10	.17	−.16	1.00	.53*	−.59*	.27**	−.28*
.20**	.26**	−.29*	.53*	1.00	−.34*	.40*	.37*
.12	−.08	−.20**	−.59*	−.34*	1.00	−.80*	−.12
−.25**	.05	.12	.27**	.40*	−.80*	1.00	.45*
.08	.25**	.11	−.28*	.37*	−.12	.45*	1.00

5. Percentage of respondents with primary social friend living in the neighborhood.
6. Percentage of respondents with the person upon whom they rely for emotional support living in the neighborhood.
7. Mean number of friends per respondent living in the neighborhood.
8. Percentage of respondents belonging to a neighborhood organization concerned about neighborhood issues.
9. Percentage of respondents belonging to other voluntary organizations located in or near the neighborhood.
10. Percentage of respondents working in the neighborhood.
11. Mean household income.
12. Percent homeownership in the neighborhood.
13. Percent black population in the neighborhood.
14. Percent neighborhood population which is Catholic.
15. Mean length of time lived in the neighborhood.
  *Statistically significant at $p = 0.01$.
 **Statistically significant at $p = 0.05$.

borhoods also have higher percentages of homeowners, participation in voluntary organizations, Catholics, church attendees, and more good friends per resident living in the neighborhood than do those neighborhoods with lower percentages of relatives. The people living in these areas have lived there, on the average, longer than people in other locations.

Best Social Friend Living in the Neighborhood. Higher percentages of respondents with their best social friend living in the neighborhood are found in those areas where residents have higher percentages of relatives living, higher percentages of providers of emotional supports, and a larger number of friends. These neighborhoods have lower incomes, higher percentages of people working in the neighborhood, and residents with longer tenure in the neighborhood than do other locations.

Providers of Emotional Supports Living in the Neighborhood. In addition to having a higher incidence of residents' relatives and best social friends residing there, neighborhoods having greater percentages of their residents' providers of emotional supports are also likely to have more friends per resident living within their boundaries and people who have lived there longer periods of time. Furthermore, these neighborhoods have a greater incidence of church attendance and more participation in voluntary organizations than do other types of areas.

Neighboring. An index was used to capture the difference in neighboring activities among the neighborhoods. It was constructed for each neighborhood by adding the respondents' scores to the survey questions concerned with the frequency of visiting, helping, borrowing from neighbors, and willingness to call on neighbors for help in an emergency and then determining the mean value. Neighboring activities occur most frequently in white, Catholic neighborhoods. These locations have higher church attendance and more friends per resident living within the neighborhood. Neighboring is also directly related to income, shopping in the neighborhood, and home-ownership.

Participation in a Neighborhood Organization. The extent of participation in organizations concerned about neighborhood issues is not related to the strength of the internal or external ties. The effectiveness or strength of the organization is the primary variable associated with participation rates (this relationship is not shown in the table, but it has a statistically significant correlation of 0.29). In addition, participation is inversely related to the relative size of the neighborhood's Catholic population and is directly related to participation in other voluntary organizations and to the homeownership rate.

Participation in Other Voluntary Organizations in the Neighborhood. Participation in other voluntary organizations (church groups, PTAs, Little League, civic, etc.) in the neighborhood occurs most frequently in neighborhoods where the residents have more relatives, a higher incidence of providers of emotional support living there, and more homeowners. Participation in these organizations is not related, statistically, to neighboring, but it is higher in neighborhoods in which residents have lived a longer period of time and where the residents have a greater number of friends.

Neighborhood Shopping. An index was used to show the extent of shopping activities in the neighborhood. It was developed for each neighborhood by adding the respondents' answers to the survey questions which dealt with the frequency of grocery shopping and shopping for small items in the neighborhood and then determining the mean value. Shopping occurs more often in white, Catholic neighborhoods, and areas having higher incomes. Neighboring also occurs more frequently in these locations.

Attending Religious Services in the Neighborhood. A high incidence of attending religious services in the neighborhood occurs in white, Catholic neighborhoods with high rates of homeownership and long-term residence. These neighborhoods have greater neighboring, more neighborhood shopping, and higher incomes, and their residents have more friends within the neighborhood than in other locations.

Place of Work. A higher percentage of residents work within their own neighborhood when it is a white neighborhood having a larger rental population. These neighborhoods are more likely to have their residents' primary social friend residing there and a greater number of friends per resident than is the case for other locations. As might be expected, neighborhoods which have more shopping facilities also have a greater percentage of their residents working within their boundaries.

Discussion

Social fabric is shown to consist of at least two distinct components. One element is formed by intimate bonds between people in the neighborhood, so-called primary ties. The other, a type of secondary relationship, is created by a more superficial form of interaction between neighbors, the neighboring that is developed through borrowing, visiting, and helping activities.

The research findings show that these two elements of social fabric are not closely related. Neighborhoods in which intimate bonds are strong do not have neighboring patterns that are as highly developed. One would not find this conclusion surprising given the choices and constraints confronting the residents in neighborhoods of different socioeconomic characteristics.

The extent to which primary ties exist in a neighborhood was analyzed in terms of relatives, best social friend, and provider of emotional supports. The different types of intimate ties are related. Neighborhoods in which a high proportion of residents reported having relatives living there are the same as those with high proportions of best social friend and provider of emotional support also residing therein. These neighborhoods also have a greater number of the residents' good friends living there.

The neighborhoods with relatively stronger primary ties differ to some extent depending upon the nature of the specific tie. The highest percentages of residents with relatives living in the neighborhood are found in Catholic neighborhoods with relatively high rates of homeowner-ship and long-term residence. Neighborhoods with high percentages of the residents with their best social friend are lower-income neighborhoods with residents having relatively longer tenure. Neighborhoods in which people's primary provider of emotional supports is more likely to reside have a high incidence of church going in the neighborhood and residents who have lived there longer on the average than other locations.

Neighborhoods with strong primary ties have something which seems to pull the residents inward. Relatives living within the neighborhood, a neighborhood church, an active voluntary organization, or a psychological investment in the neighborhood on the part of the resident through long tenure are some of the factors which are related to the presence of best social friend, provider of emotional supports, and a large number of friends in the neighborhood.

Higher incomes provide a pull in a different direction. The prevalence of intimate ties in a neighborhood is associated in a negative manner with the economic level of that area. The median income of the neighborhood is inversely related to the incidence of relatives, best social friend, provider of emotional supports, and number of friends living in the neighborhood, although the relationship is only statistically significant for the best social friend variable.

Lack of economic resources limits people's mobility. It lessens people's choices with respect to where they can afford to live, and it decreases their day-to-day options for going outside of the neighborhood to socialize and to maintain intimate relationships. It is therefore not surprising to see that intimate ties are more prevalent in poorer neighborhoods. Poorer people have fewer resources with which to maintain long-distance relationships. However, this does not mean that the intimate relationships in poorer neighborhoods are necessarily stronger than the intimate ties that exist outside of the neighborhood for residents of higher-income neighborhoods. In fact, there is reason to believe that the ties in poorer neighborhoods are less strong. Because lack of income limits choice, the pool of people from whom to choose best social friend and provider of emotional supports is smaller for those with less income. Therefore, the help and satisfactions derived from these relationships may be less for those in the lower-income groups (also the magnitude of their problems may be greater). This may explain, in part, why levels of life satisfaction and happiness are lower in these neighborhoods. (This discussion is elaborated upon in Chapters 8 and 9.)

The frequency with which neighboring occurs varies directly with income and it occurs to the greatest extent in white, homeownership neighborhoods with a high proportion of Catholics who attend religious services in a neighborhood church and who also shop in the neighborhood. Neighborhoods having most of these characteristics and not falling into the high-income ranges may be thought of as the traditional ethnic community, a place in which people are bound together by a common religious background which ties them to the neighborhood. As the income level rises and residents are less constrained geographically by a lack of income, they form and maintain intimate ties outside of the neighborhood as well.

Participation in other forms of neighborhood life depends to some extent on the characteristics of the neighborhood and the strength of the internal ties. Participation in voluntary neighborhood organizations of all types is highest in neighborhoods with high homeownership rates. Again, this follows from the choice-constraint perspective. Homeowners have a financial stake in the neighborhood and therefore could be expected to have a greater incentive to participate in the affairs of the neighborhood. Participation in voluntary organizations (identified as those not concerned exclusively with neighborhood issues) is highest in neighborhoods in which primary ties are stronger. The strength of these ties serves to pull people together, and it is not surprising to find greater participation in these neighborhoods than in those where external ties are relatively stronger.

The social fabric of the neighborhood is most vulnerable in neighborhoods that have high transiency rates. Neighborhoods in which population turnover is high (low average number of years lived in the neighborhood) are less likely to have strong primary ties, neighborhood religious institutions, or voluntary organizations within their boundaries. Furthermore, if these neighborhoods are lower-income, the neighborhood aspects of social fabric will be weaker. Therefore, highly transient, lower-income neighborhoods not only will lack the economic and institutional base for dealing with neighborhood concerns but will have relatively weaker internal social relationships as well.

In order to gain additional insights into some of the relationships discussed in this section, we placed neighborhoods into one of four groups, depending upon the internal strength of their primary relationships. This typology was then used to study how other variables changed with variations in the strength of a neighborhood group's primary ties. The analysis is shown in Table 19, and the results generally agree with those of the correlation analysis; however, a few differences are observed because of variations among the neighborhoods within each of the groups.

Neighborhoods in which primary ties are the strongest are those that have been previously described as the white, Catholic, ethnic neighborhoods. Worship is more likely to occur within these areas, neighboring occurs more frequently, homeownership is high, mean years lived in the neighborhood is the highest of any group, and neighborhood attachment is higher than in the other locations.

The neighborhoods in this group are unique. The residents are more embedded in the fabric of the social life of the neighborhood than they are in other neighborhood groups. This is most likely a result of the strong church base which pulls the residents inward and gains their commitments.

The neighborhood group having the weakest internal primary ties has the highest income, the lowest homeownership rate, and the lowest resident tenure. Resident satisfaction is high.

Table 19. Selected Variables for Neighborhoods Grouped by the
Strength of Their Primary Ties

| | Strength of primary ties[a] | | | |
| | Strongest | | Weakest | |
Variable	1	2	3	4
Percentage with relatives in neighborhood	62	50	38	25
Percentage with best social friend in neighborhood	63	58	52	46
Percentage with person closest to in neighborhood	42	35	27	23
Percentage doing main grocery shopping in or near neighborhood	73	69	68	78
Percentage worshipping in or near neighborhood	68	56	48	46
Percentage borrowing sometimes or often from neighbors	31	25	26	27
Percentage helping or being helped by neighbors	70	60	58	56

(continued)

[a]The neighborhood groups were constructed by creating a neighborhood index which added together the responses to the following questions for the residents in each neighborhood: (a) Do you have relatives living in this neighborhood? (No = 1; Yes = 2); (b) Where does the person you visit most often live? (In your neighborhood, say within a 10-minute walk = 2; all other responses = 1); and (c) Where does the person you are closest to live (excluding spouse)? (coded as above). The mean value of the index for each neighborhood was determined by dividing the total by the number of respondents.

The index was standardized as follows:

$$Zi = \frac{Ci - \overline{C}}{\sigma}$$

The differences among the four groups can be explained in terms of the choice-constraint framework. Residents in the weak primary-tie group have the greatest economic choice and hence are more likely to have ties outside the neighborhood and would not be expected to be as

Table 19. (continued)

Variable	Strongest		Weakest	
	1	2	3	4
Percentage of homeownership	74	66	64	41
Percentage of blacks	3	27	30	11
Percentage of Catholics	71	48	38	38
Percentage strongly attached to neighborhood	70	65	60	59
Percentage rating neighborhood good or excellent	79	68	69	80
Percentage not too happy with life	15	20	20	14
Percentage satisfied with life	87	85	85	87
Mean household income	$13,670	$12,290	$12,910	$14,790
Mean years lived in neighborhood	28	24	19	14

(Header spanning: "Strength of primary ties[a]")

where Z_i = standardized normal value of the index for neighborhood i, C_i = value of the index for neighborhood i, $\overline{C}$ = mean value of the index for all neighborhoods, and σ = standard deviation of the index distribution for all neighborhoods.

The neighborhood groups were created as follows:

Z Group	All neighborhoods with Z scores in the range:
1 (strongest primary ties in neighborhood)	1.01 and above
2	0 to 1.00
3	−.001 to −1.00
4 (weakest primary ties in neighborhood)	Less than −1.01

strongly bound to the neighborhood as residents in other groups. Similarly, resident satisfaction with the neighborhood as a place to live should be high, or the residents would exercise their greater choice and move.

Residents in the strongest primary-tie group, even

though their income is not significantly less than that in the weakest tie group, are the most committed to their neighborhood. This is explained by the stronger religious institutional structure and by the greater homogeneity of the residents in the strong-tie group.

This analysis illustrates the importance of the interaction between the neighborhood and the residents in creating the social structure of the neighborhood. Neighborhoods that offer strong rewards for participation—as exemplified by the strong-tie group—will create a more durable social fabric and sense of attachment than neighborhoods in which the lure for internal involvement is not so strong.

RELATIONSHIP TO NEIGHBORHOOD ATTITUDES

Table 20 shows correlations at the neighborhood level between neighborhood attachment (very strongly attached . . . not at all attached) and satisfaction (rating of neighborhood as a place to live), and all of the socioeconomic and social-fabric variables discussed earlier in the chapter. The results show that the feeling of attachment is higher in neighborhoods in which intimate ties are stronger.

Neighborhood Attachment

Neighborhood attachment is greater in neighborhoods in which residents are more apt to shop, go to church, have relatives, and have their best social friend or provider of emotional supports. Neighboring is higher in these neighborhoods; residents have more friends living there and have lived there for longer periods of time; work performed in the neighborhood is more common; and participation in neighborhood organizations occurs more frequently. These neighborhoods also have more homeownership and a larger Catholic population than the others.

Table 20. Correlations between Selected Variables and Attitudes about the Neighborhood[a]

	Attachment	Satisfaction
Shopping	.20**	.38*
Worship	.39*	.37*
Neighboring	.36*	.60*
Percentage with relatives in neighborhood	.30*	−.07
Percentage with best social friend in neighborhood	.28*	−.18
Percentage with provider of emotional support in neighborhood	.24**	−.08
Mean number of friends in neighborhood	.41*	−.04
Percentage belonging to neighborhood organizations	.41*	.16
Percentage belonging to voluntary organizations	.19	.18
Percentage who work in neighborhood	.21**	−.04
Mean income	.06	.83*
Percentage of homeownership	.41*	.47*
Percentage of blacks	−.16	−.65*
Percentage of Catholics	.26**	.40*
Mean years living in neighborhood	.52*	−.11
Attachment[b]	1.00	.36*
Satisfaction[c]	.36*	1.00

[a]The analysis was performed for all 74 neighborhoods.
[b]Question: When you think of your attachment to this neighborhood, are you very strongly attached, strongly attached, undecided, not strongly attached, or not at all attached?; coded 1–5 with higher values showing stronger attachment.
[c]Question: In general, how would you rate this neighborhood as a place to live?; coded 1–4 with 1 = Poor, 4 = Excellent.
*Statistically significant at $p = 0.01$.
**Statistically significant at $p = 0.05$.

Satisfaction

Higher satisfaction levels are found in neighborhoods having higher income levels. These locations are predominantly white and Catholic and have higher homeownership rates. Neighboring activities occur at levels above those of other locations, and utilization of neighborhood facilities for worship and shopping occurs at higher rates.

Attachment is higher in neighborhoods in which people's primary ties are stronger, homeownership is high, and where term of residence is relatively long. People in these neighborhoods experience a stronger emotional commitment to the neighborhood, and therefore attachment and loyalty to it exceed the levels reached in those neighborhoods where residents' external ties are stronger. Strong external relationships, existing in predominantly higher-income areas, tend to lower the need for residents to rely on their neighbors for social and emotional supports.

Satisfaction levels are higher in neighborhoods in which residents' potential economic mobility is the greatest—the same types of neighborhoods in which attachment is apt to be lower. Satisfaction is also related to a number of the same variables as is attachment, such as shopping, neighboring, percentage of Catholics, churchgoing, and homeownership. Therefore, there is an element of satisfaction that is similar to attachment and this is the reason for the correlation of 0.36 between these two variables.

The social fabric of the neighborhood relates in different ways to the feelings that people have about their place of residence. Satisfaction is related more to the economic level and less to the presence of primary ties (except in the ethnic neighborhoods), whereas attachment more closely depends upon the strength of the ties that exist among the residents within the neighborhood.

The racial composition of the neighborhood is not related to attachment, but it is related to satisfaction. Residents are increasingly less satisfied with their neighborhood as a place to live as the percent of black population rises; however, this may be a result of the contextual influences discussed in Chapter 8.

RELATIONSHIP TO LIFE HAPPINESS AND LIFE SATISFACTION

Table 21 shows correlations of the life happiness and life satisfaction variables with the variables discussed in

Table 21. Life Happiness and Life Satisfaction Variables
Correlated with Selected Variables[a]

	Life happiness	Life satisfaction
Shopping	.39*	.33*
Worship	.32*	.25**
Neighboring	.65*	.68*
Percentage with relatives in neighborhood	−.09	−.20**
Percentage with social friend in neighborhood	−.14	−.20**
Percentage with provider of emotional support in neighborhood	−.06	−.17
Mean number of friends in neighborhood	.07	.15
Percentage belonging to neighborhood organizations	.26*	.12
Percentage belonging to voluntary organizations	.18	.17
Percentage who work in neighborhood	.16	.11
Mean income	.73*	.57*
Percentage of homeownership	.41*	.33*
Percentage of blacks	−.66*	−.50*
Percentage of Catholics	.38*	.31*
Mean years living in neighborhood	−.10	−.14
Attachment	.31*	.21**
Neighborhood satisfaction	.80*	.50*
Life happiness[b]	1.00	.65*
Life satisfaction[c]	.65*	1.00

[a]The analysis was performed for all 74 neighborhoods.
[b]Question: Taking all things together, how would you say things are these days—
would you say you are very happy, pretty happy, or not too happy? Higher values
show greater happiness.
[c]Question: In general, are you very satisfied, satisfied, neither satisfied nor dissatisfied, dissatisfied, or very dissatisfied with your life as a whole these days? High values show greater satisfaction.
*Statistically significant at $p = 0.01$.
**Statistically significant at $p = 0.05$.

the other sections of this chapter. Neighborhoods in which
life happiness is higher are those in which the residents
shop and attend church more frequently, neighbor more
often, and participate in neighborhood issue organizations
at higher rates. These neighborhoods are generally white,

Catholic, homeownership areas with higher income and higher levels of neighborhood satisfaction and attachment.

Life satisfaction is greater in the same types of neighborhoods. Further, the level of life satisfaction in the neighborhood is inversely related to having social friends, relatives, and providers of emotional supports (not significant at $p = 0.05$) living in the neighborhood.

The correlation analysis shows that intimate personal relationships within the neighborhood are not related statistically to life happiness and are related in a negative manner to life satisfaction. That is, life happiness is not higher in neighborhoods in which the residents are more likely to have relatives, best social friend, and provider of emotional supports living there, and life satisfaction is actually lower in these locations. However, as Table 19 shows, this is not true for all types of neighborhoods. The ethnic neighborhoods show higher levels of life happiness than many of the weaker primary tie neighborhoods.

The neighborhoods in which life happiness and life satisfaction are highest are those in which neighboring is also high. The people in these neighborhoods have greater life choices—their income is higher and they make greater use of the neighborhood for shopping, worship, and participation in organizations.

This suggests, as did Chapter 2, that people's feelings about life in general do not necessarily depend upon the strength of their neighborhood personal networks. People's personal networks are not constrained by the geographic boundaries of the neighborhood. Their social support systems emanate outward from the neighborhood, and people having more options appear to be happier.

This does not mean that neighborhood is not important. It does provide outlets for neighboring, participation, shopping, and worship which offer certain kinds of supports and conveniences to the residents. The location of the intimate ties, however, is not critical to a person's life happiness and satisfaction—at least so long as that individual can avail himself or herself of the supports when needed, and this is clearly demonstrated by the high levels of life satisfaction shown in both the strongest and weakest primary-tie neighborhood groups in Table 19.

It is not possible to conclude from this research that intimate neighborhood ties are not important to one's feelings about life. In lower-income neighborhoods the residents do not have so great an opportunity to maintain external ties and internal ties are more prevalent. These relationships could be of extreme importance to the mental health of the residents. Although the research shows that in some neighborhoods in which these ties are stronger life happiness and satisfaction are likely to be lower, this does not necessarily mean that intimate ties are not providing significant psychological supports. Lower-income individuals are confronted by a number of difficult situations, all of which may lead to fewer positive feelings about life. The personal neighborhood networks that exist could be providing strong support in the face of very severe, psychologically depressing forces.

The research shows that individuals in poorer, often black neighborhoods, in which homeownership is low, report less life happiness and less life satisfaction than those living in other types of neighborhoods. Some of these poorer neighborhoods, fortunately, have stronger intimate personal networks than some less poor areas. Therefore, there is a structure within these areas that is available to the residents to help them cope with stress. (Chapter 9 will show that this does not apply to all low-income neighborhoods.)

DISCUSSION

It is not possible to conclude from this analysis that there is a cause-and-effect relationship between any of the dimensions of social fabric and people's attitudes about the neighborhood, their feelings about life, or the long-term stability of the neighborhood. Some of the elements of social fabric, however, were shown to be associated with higher levels of attachment (neighboring and the strength of primary ties), neighborhood satisfaction (neighboring), life happiness (neighboring and primary ties in white, Catholic neighborhoods), and life satisfaction (neighboring).

There are a number of variables associated with neighborhood attitudes and feelings about life. These include variables which describe amenities, such as shopping and the presence of religious institutions, and characteristics of the residents themselves. Neighborhoods in which the residents frequently shop and worship are usually the same ones in which the residents express higher levels of attachment, satisfaction, happiness, and life satisfaction. The availability and use of these institutions in the neighborhood can be viewed as increasing the convenience of the neighborhood for the residents as well as providing a focal point for increasing the contact among neighborhood residents.

The income level of the neighborhood is directly related to the residents' attitudes about their life and their satisfaction with the neighborhood. Higher incomes give the residents greater choice in terms of where to live and with whom to associate. It is not surprising that higher-income individuals choose to live in areas that are convenient to shopping, religious institutions, and the like. Neighboring is also more frequent in many higher-income areas.

Neighborhoods in which a greater percentage of the population is Catholic display higher levels of attachment, satisfaction, happiness, and life satisfaction. This is consistent with other results because these areas also are likely to have higher levels of income, homeownership, and neighboring.

The racial composition of the neighborhood is associated with most of these attitudinal variables. Neighborhoods having a high percentage of black residents are likely to show low levels of neighborhood satisfaction, life happiness, and life satisfaction. As neighborhoods become increasingly black, they are less likely to have facilities for shopping and church-going and the income and homeownership levels are likely to be lower. Neighboring occurs at lower levels in these locations.

This analysis shows that a number of variables are interrelated. However, income and religion seem to stand out. Residents of neighborhoods in which income is lower may be expected to have fewer positive feelings about a number of different things. However, this does not mean that lower-income neighborhoods are vulnerable to unwanted change, mental health problems, or lack of commitment on the part of residents. As the income level of the neighborhood declines, the strength of the primary ties within the neighborhood becomes stronger (but not as strong as in the ethnic neighborhoods); and it is the strength of these primary ties, among other factors, that contributes to the feelings of attachment felt by the residents for their neighborhoods.

As income falls, residents become more dependent upon place to satisfy their needs. The neighborhoods which become most likely to decline are those in which other supportive elements of the neighborhood environment are lacking or have ceased to exist. The lack of neighborhood institutions for shopping and worship removes potential strengths. Areas in which transiency is high do not provide a climate conducive to forming strong intimate bonds or neighborhood attachments. The research shows that social fabric can be strong in a number of different types of neighborhoods but that its components differ. As the neighborhood income level falls, primary ties become stronger within the neighborhood, but the pressures of coping that are forced on these relationships rise because access to providers of support who are not in the neighborhood is diminished.

The findings described in this chapter are consistent with the choice-constraint framework and the concept of the community of limited liability, discussed in Chapters 1 and 2, respectively. As income rises, neighborhood residents are more likely to maintain strong primary relationships outside the neighborhood. However, this does not mean that attachment cannot be high in these neighborhoods. The feelings that residents have toward the neighborhood depend upon what the neighborhood has to offer them in return for making a commitment in terms of time, money, and emotions to their surroundings. Neighborhoods offer their residents opportunities for interpersonal interactions, service consumption, and participation. When these are available and valued—as in the Catholic neighborhoods—the residents are likely to make investments in the neighborhood and report higher levels of attachment. It is thus the strength of the social fabric and the availability of neighborhood-based institutions that create a community of mutual self-interest out of which arise the residents' attachments to the area.

CHAPTER 7

Social Fabric and Neighborhood Change

INTRODUCTION

Chapter 6 showed that there is a direct relationship between the social fabric of the neighborhood and the feelings that people have about where they live. Although there are differences in the ways in which various elements of social fabric relate to respondents' neighborhood feelings of attachment and satisfaction or to their feelings toward life in general, a number of the social fabric variables were shown to relate positively to these feelings.

In this chapter, the link between the social fabric of the neighborhood and neighborhood change is examined in detail. Neighborhood change can be analyzed in a number of ways. It could be defined socially in terms of the characteristics of the respondents; economically in terms of household income or property values; structurally in terms of the uses made of the residential, institutional, and commercial property; or in terms of the quality of life.[1]

[1]For a discussion of the factors contributing to neighborhood change, see Roger S. Ahlbrandt, Jr., and Paul Brophy, *Neighborhood Revitalization: Theory and Practice* (Lexington, Ma.: Lexington Books, 1975), Ch. 2–4; Roger S. Ahlbrandt, Jr., and James V. Cunningham, *A New Public Policy for Neighborhood Preservation* (New York: Praeger, 1979), Ch. 3; Anthony Downs, *Neighborhoods, Urban Development and Public Policies* (Washington, D.C.: Brookings Institution, 1981); John M. Goering,

This chapter takes an economic perspective. Neighborhood change is defined in economic terms and the appreciation in residential real estate prices over time is used to
monitor the relative economic health of the area. Theorists
describing housing markets have shown that housing market prices capture all facets of a neighborhood's environment and that therefore prices can be used to measure the
market's composite valuation of the neighborhood and all
of its elements at a given point in time.[2] A time series of

"Neighborhood Tipping and Racial Transitions: A Review of Social Science Evidence," *Journal of the American Institute of Planners* 44 (January
1968): 68–78; Rolf Goetze, *Building Neighborhood Confidence* (Cambridge, Ma.: Ballinger, 1976); William C. Grigsby and Louis Rosenberg,
Urban Housing Policy (New York: APS Publications, 1975); Charles L.
Leven, James T. Little, Hugh O. Nourse, and R. B. Read, *Neighborhood
Change: Lessons in the Dynamics of Urban Decay* (New York: Praeger,
1976); Public Affairs Counseling, *The Dynamics of Neighborhood
Change* (Washington, D.C.: U.S. Government Printing Office, 1975); Real
Estate Research Corporation, *Analysis of Data on Neighborhood Preser-
vation Program Areas* (Chicago: Real Estate Research Corp., 1976);
Michael Stegman, *Housing Investment in the Inner City: The Dynamics
of Decline* (Cambridge, Ma.: The MIT Press, 1972); George Sternlieb, *The
Urban Housing Dilemma* (New York: New York City Housing Development Administration, 1972); George Sternlieb and R. W. Burchell, *Residential Abandonment: The Tenement Landlord Revisited* (New Brunswick, N. J.: Rutgers University Press, 1973); and Robert K. Yin,
Conserving America's Neighborhoods (New York: Plenum Press, 1982).
[2]A discussion of urban housing markets is contained in David L. Birch,
Eric S. Brown, Richard P. Coleman, Delores W. DaLomba, William L. Par-
sons, Linda C. Sharpe, and Sheryll A. Weber, *A Behavioral Model of
Neighborhood Change* (Boston: Joint Center for Urban Studies of the Massachusetts Institute of Technology and Harvard University, 1977); David
L. Birch *et al.*, *The Community Analysis Model* (Boston: Joint Center for
Urban Studies of the Massachusetts Institute of Technology and Harvard
University, 1977); Katherine Bradbury, "Housing Supply Policies: An
Examination of Partial Equilibrium Impacts in a Metropolitan Area," Dis-
cussion Paper, #418–77 (Madison, Wi.: University of Wisconsin, Insti-
tute for Research on Poverty, 1977); Frank DeLeeuw, "The Distribution
of Housing Services: A Mathematical Model," Working Paper No. 208–1
(Washington, D.C.: Urban Institute, November 1971); Frank DeLeeuw
and Raymond J. Struyk, *The Web of Urban Housing* (Washington, D.C.:
The Urban Institute, 1975); Gregory K. Ingram, John F. Kain, and Royce
J. Ginn, *Detroit Prototype of the NBER Urban Simulation Model* (New
York: National Bureau of Economic Research, 1972); John F. Kain and

residential real estate prices, then, can be used to measure changes in the neighborhood over time in terms of the market's perception of the value of its combined attributes.

An analysis of neighborhood change from the standpoint of real estate prices runs the risk of masking or ignoring the impact of price changes on the current resident population. A neighborhood experiencing high rates of price increase may pose significant economic problems for lower-income renters and homeowners; and the displacement of individuals from a neighborhood because of a rapid increase in rents or property taxes or the conversion of property from one use to another may impose social costs as well, if existing neighborhood-based social support systems are disrupted.

The analysis in this chapter does not take the position that higher rates of price increase are better than lower rates. It merely uses the price-appreciation variable as a means for analyzing the social fabric and institutional characteristics of the neighborhoods associated with variations in the rate at which the economic value of the neighborhood is changing.

THE MODEL

The model that is being used to guide the analysis is shown in Figure 3. It posits neighborhood change to be a function of the institutions that serve the neighborhocd, the level of economic resources in the neighborhood, and the strength of the social fabric. On the assumption that people have choices about where to live and participate,

John M. Quigley, *Housing Markets and Racial Discrimination: A Microeconomic Analysis* (New York: National Bureau of Economic Research, 1975); Richard F. Muth, *Cities and Housing* (Chicago: University of Chicago Press, 1969); Mahlon R. Straszheim, *An Econometric Analysis of the Urban Housing Market* (New York: National Bureau of Economic Research, 1975); and Raymond J. Struyk, Sue A. Marshall, and Larry J. Ozanne, *Housing Policies for the Urban Poor* (Washington, D.C.: The Urban Institute, 1978).

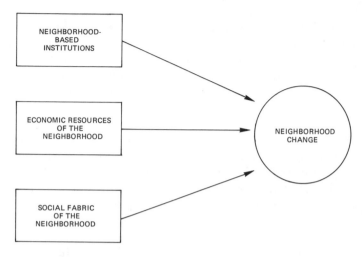

Figure 3. Factors influencing neighborhood change.

the neighborhoods which will be economically the strongest are those having attributes that are in the greatest
demand. These neighborhoods include those with good
physical facilities, adequate services, and a desirable social
fabric as well as those in which residents have sufficient
resources to maintain the housing stock. This model is very
simple, and it is only being used as a framework for inves-
tigating a few general relationships, particularly the relative importance of the social fabric variables.

A more complete model would recognize that there are
a number of other factors which affect the economic health
of the neighborhood. These include overall trends in job
generation and the location of economic activity; population shifts; willingness of lenders to extend credit and the
terms upon which it is made available; perceptions of real-
tors toward the neighborhood; racial and socioeconomic
trends in the neighborhood and the areas surrounding it;
major institutional change such as the expansion of a hos-
pital, closing of a public school or contraction of a business
commercial area; the age of the housing and its architec-

tural features; relative proximity of the neighborhood to cultural activities, recreation, jobs; and so on.[3]

The analysis being performed in this section is incomplete in the sense that only a few of the many factors influencing neighborhood change are being examined. However, that does not mean that the results of such analysis will necessarily be suspect. The purpose of this exercise is to test for the relationship between neighborhood change and the three sets of variables shown in Figure 3. If these relationships are strong, this should be evident from a simple correlation analysis of these variables for all of Pittsburgh's neighborhoods having a residential real estate market. This investigation is meant to be suggestive and not conclusive.

ANALYSIS

The residential real estate price data were available for all residential real estate transactions (1–4 unit structures) in every neighborhood in the city of Pittsburgh for the period 1973–1979. A two-year weighted average was used in order to smooth out random fluctuations and the percentage rate of change in sales prices was computed for the period 1975–1979. In order for this variable to reflect changes in the valuation placed on the neighborhood, and not changes in the distribution of houses for sale, the distribution of homes available for sale must be relatively constant from one year to the next. This assumption is valid for Pittsburgh. There has been very little new single-family construction in the city during the last ten years. In addition, the analysis is performed at the neighborhood level; Pittsburgh's neighborhoods are relatively small (2,500 housing units on the average) and most of the housing stock in each neighborhood is of similar age and construction.

[3]See Footnote 2.

Sixty-seven of Pittsburgh's 74 neighborhoods were selected for analysis. The excluded neighborhoods were those with little single-family housing. These included the central business district, commercial districts, and public housing communities.

Table 22 shows that the percentage rate of increase in real estate prices is directly related to the use of neighborhood facilities for shopping, the mean housing value in 1979, and the percent of the population that is white. Thus, the presence of a commercial base in or near the neighborhood, and the economic level of the neighborhood, are strongly associated with the economic health of the area's real estate market. This is consistent with what housing-market theory would suggest. The demand for housing is responsive to the income level of the residents and the relative attractiveness of the neighborhood with respect to the availability of shopping and other services. The percentage of whites variable is associated statistically with the other two variables and is probably capturing some of their effects. The various dimensions of social fabric are not related in a statistically significant manner.

To test the sensitivity of this conclusion to the length of the time period over which the real estate price change variable was computed, a similar analysis was conducted for a two-year time span (1977–1979), and the results are shown in Table 23. The variable, percentage of change in real estate prices (1977–1979), is directly related to the prevalence of shopping in the neighborhood, neighboring activities, participation in neighborhood organizations, and the attachment of residents to the neighborhood. Price changes over two years, therefore, vary with the level of interaction and participation of the residents. However, as the time period is extended, the social fabric-related variables lose their power to explain relative differences in the strength of the real estate market.

In order to investigate the effects of social fabric, if any, in more detail, income differences among neighborhoods were partially controlled for by selecting only those neigh-

Table 22. Percentage Change in Neighborhood Real Estate Prices
(1975–1979) Correlated with Selected Variables[a]

| | Correlation coefficients—Real estate price change 1975–1979 | |
	All neighborhoods (67)[b]	Neighborhoods having mean income less than city-wide mean (33)[c]
Shopping	.33	.39**
Worship	.08	.22
Neighboring	.05	.10
Percentage with relatives in the neighborhood	.07	.20
Percentage with best social friend in neighborhood	.01	−.03
Percentage with provider of emotional support in neighborhood	−.15	−.21
Mean number of friends in neighborhood	−.06	−.02
Percentage belonging to neighborhood organizations	.13	.21
Percentage belonging to voluntary organizations	.12	.22
Percentage who work in neighborhood	.12	.29**
Mean income	.04	.16
Value	.25**	.58*
Percentage of homeownership	−.14	−.13
Percentage of blacks	−.25**	−.41*
Percentage of Catholics	.19	.31**
Mean years living in neighborhood	.02	.13
Attachment	.07	.21
Satisfaction	.13	.28
Loyalty	.18	.27

[a]For a description of the variables, see Table 25.
[b]67 neighborhoods.
[c]33 neighborhoods.
* Statistically significant at $p = 0.01$.
** Statistically significant at $p = 0.05$.

Table 23. Percentage Change in Neighborhood Real Estate Prices
(1977–1979) Correlated with Selected Variables[a]

	Correlation coefficients—Real estate price change 1977–1979	
	All neighborhoods (67)[b]	Neighborhoods having mean income less than city-wide mean (33)[c]
Shopping	.33*	.34**
Worship	.18	.39**
Neighboring	.23**	.50*
Percentage with relatives in neighborhood	−.06	−.01
Percentage with best social friend in neighborhood	−.14	−.29**
Percentage with provider of emotional support in neighborhood	−.23**	−.32**
Mean number of friends	.08	.10
Percentage belonging to neighborhood organizations	.21**	.28
Percentage belonging to voluntary organizations	.16	.26
Percentage who work in neighborhood	.09	.06
Mean income	−.10	.09
Value	.06	.13
Percentage of homeownership	−.11	.06
Percentage of blacks	−.04	−.18
Percentage of Catholics	.02	.13
Mean years living in neighborhood	.04	.15
Attachment	.22**	.32**
Satisfaction	.01	.18
Loyalty	−.01	.01

[a]For a description of the variables, see Table 25.
[b]67 neighborhoods.
[c]33 neighborhoods.
*Statistically significant at $p = 0.01$.
**Statistically significant at $p = 0.05$.

borhoods with mean household income less than the city-wide mean. This was done on the assumption that social fabric may be more important to the health of lower-income neighborhoods (Chapter 9 discusses this in detail), and that the relationship between differences in the strength of social fabric and real estate price change may have become obscured when all of the neighborhoods were included in the analysis.

LOWER-INCOME NEIGHBORHOODS

Table 22 also shows the correlations between the real estate price change variable and the selected variables for the 33 neighborhoods having a mean household income less than that for the city and a significant residential real estate market. The conclusions are similar in many respects to the city-wide analysis. Real estate prices have increased to the greatest extent in white, Catholic neighborhoods with shopping facilities nearby and a high percentage of the population working in the neighborhood. Attachment and satisfaction were higher in the neighborhoods experiencing greater rates of price appreciation, but the correlations were not statistically significant ($p = 0.05$). Larger price changes were also found in neighborhoods having higher residential real estate values.

Interestingly, neither variations in neighboring nor differences in the prevalence of primary ties among residents in the neighborhoods are related to the price change variable in a systematic manner. This is also shown in Table 24, where the neighborhoods are grouped into the following five categories based upon their percentage rates of price change:

- Group 1. Price change greater than one standard deviation above the city mean rate of increase
- Group 2. Price change up to one standard deviation above the city-wide mean

Table 24. Relationship between Selected Social Fabric Variables and Residential Real Estate Prices

Percentage change in residential real estate prices (number of neighborhoods)[a]	Percentage of total respondents in each group			Neighboring percentage often or sometimes		
	Relatives in neighborhood	Best social friend in neighborhood	Provider of emotional supports in neighborhood	Borrowing	Visiting	Helping
Group 1 (9)	48%	56%	32%	24%	46%	56%
Group 2 (6)	50	60	34	21	48	57
Group 3 (12)	53	60	36	21	48	58
Group 4 (6)	37	54	31	18	41	52
Group 5 (6)	36	57	27	21	47	56

[a]Neighborhoods were categorized into groups for analytical purposes based upon their relative rates of price change for the period 1975–1979. Standardized scores were computed for each neighborhood using the formula shown below and four groups were constructed with Z scores in the ranges indicated under the formula. The fifth group consists of all other neighborhoods having mean household income less than the city-wide mean and no significant residential real estate market.

$$Z_i = \frac{P_i - \overline{P}}{\sigma}$$

where Z_i = Z score for i^{th} neighborhood, P_i = percentage rate of price increase for single family homes (1–4 unit structures) in the ith neighborhood during the period 1975–1979, $\overline{P}$ = mean rate of price increase for single-family homes in the city during the period 1975–1979, and σ = standard deviation. Z score range for Group 1 is above 1.0; for Group 2, 0 to 1.0; for Group 3, −1.0 to less than 0; for Group 4, less than −1.0.

- Group 3. Price change less than one standard deviation below the city mean
- Group 4. Price change more than one standard deviation below the city mean
- Group 5. Neighborhoods with very few real estate transactions

Except for one variable—the percentage of respondents with relatives living in the neighborhood—there are no large variations in the values of the social-fabric variables across the price change groups. This indicates that, at least for this method of categorizing neighborhoods, the social-fabric variables are more or less invariant among groups. Social fabric, in terms of primary ties and neighboring activities, therefore, is equally strong or at least equally prevalent in all of these categories.

The correlation analysis was repeated using the two-year price-change variable (Table 23), and the results show that this variable varies directly with shopping, worship, neighboring, and attachment and varies inversely with the incidence of best social friend and provider of emotional supports living in the neighborhood. Except for the negative relationships, these results paralleled those for all 67 neighborhoods. The negative relationship between the neighborhood location of the two providers of social support and the price-change variable is not surprising if one considers the fact that these two elements of social support have higher values in poorer neighborhoods and in areas where the use of neighborhood facilities and neighboring occur less often. Therefore, these dimensions of the neighborhoods' social fabric are capturing the inverse effects of a number of other relationships which relate strongly to the strength of the neighborhoods' real estate market.

DISCUSSION

The link between certain elements of social fabric and economic change in the neighborhood, as measured in

Table 25. Description of the Variables

1. Shopping = The index was constructed by adding the respondent's answer to the survey questions which asked (1) how often do you do your main grocery shopping in or near your neighborhood, and (2) how often do you use stores in your neighborhood for shopping for small items, dry cleaning, etc. The questions were coded on a four-point scale (1 = none, 4 = all). Higher values of the index show increased neighborhood shopping.

2. Worship = Survey question: How often do you attend religious services in or near your neighborhood? (coded as above). Higher values show greater frequency of worship in or near the neighborhood.

3. Neighboring = The index was constructed by summing and weighting equally answers to the following four survey questions: frequency of borrowing or exchanging things with neighbors, frequency of visiting neighbors, frequency of helping (or being helped by) neighbors with small tasks, and willingness to call on neighbors for help in an emergency. The borrowing, visiting and helping questions were coded on a 4-point scale, with higher values showing more frequent neighboring; the emergency question was coded Yes = 1; No = 0. Higher values of the index show more frequent neighboring.

4. Percentage of respondents with relatives living in the neighborhood.

5. Percentage of respondents with best social friend living in the neighborhood.

6. Percentage of respondents with the person upon whom they rely for emotional support living in the neighborhood.

7. Mean number of friends per respondent living in the neighborhood.

8. Percentage of respondents belonging to a neighborhood organization concerned about neighborhood issues.

9. Percentage of respondents belonging to other voluntary organizations located in or near the neighborhood.

10. Percentage of respondents working in the neighborhood.

11. Mean household income.

12. Mean value of residential property in the neighborhood, based on actual sale prices of single family residences (1–4 units) during 1979.

13. Percentage of homeownership in the neighborhood.

14. Percentage black population in the neighborhood.

15. Percentage of neighborhood population which is Catholic.

16. Mean length of time lived in the neighborhood.

17. Attachment = Question: When you think of your attachment to this neighborhood, are you very strongly attached, strongly attached, undecided, not strongly attached, or not at all attached? Coded 1–5 with higher values showing stronger attachment.

18. Satisfaction = Question: In general, how would you rate this neighborhood as a place to live? Coded 1–4 with 1 = Poor, 4 = Excellent.

19. Loyalty = Question: Does your neighborhood claim a greater loyalty from you than the rest of the city? Coded No = 0; Yes = 1.

20. Real estate price change = Percentage of change in residential real estate prices 1975–1979 (or 1977–1979 where indicated).

terms of real estate prices, is apparent in this analysis only in the very short run. The overall economic level of the neighborhood and the availability and use of neighborhood facilities for shopping are more closely aligned with the direction of movement of the real estate market over a longer time period.

This does not mean that social fabric is not an important consideration in understanding the whole question of neighborhood change. Chapter 3 showed that people's attitudes toward the neighborhood in terms of attachment and satisfaction are related to neighboring and to some of the variables capturing the strength of primary ties in the neighborhood. To the extent that these attitudes lead to behavior which helps to make the neighborhood a better place to live, it is reasonable to argue that the strength of social fabric has an indirect effect upon the social and economic health of the neighborhood.

Part of the difficulty in trying to measure economic change in the neighborhood may lie in the selection of the real estate price-change variable as the appropriate indicator. The assumption underlying the selection of this variable was that economic change must be viewed over time and that real estate prices capture all facets of neighborhood change, including the economic aspects. It was further assumed that neighborhood social fabric does not change very quickly and therefore data showing differences in the social fabric of the neighborhood at one point in time would serve as a good proxy for the differences that existed among the neighborhoods at any point in time during the four-year time span selected for analysis. This latter assumption was based upon observations of Pittsburgh's neighborhoods during the 1970s and the impression that rapid racial and socioeconomic change was not occurring.

Finally, there are many other factors which influence the housing market, and therefore the effect of social fabric may be masked by these other variables. Thus, it may not be surprising that a direct link between the strength of the social fabric and the stability of the real estate market over time is not observable. Real estate price changes are a gross measure of neighborhood change and may simply not be able to capture the slow, subtle effects of differences in strengths and weaknesses of the neighborhood's social fabric, effects which are observed in the attitudinal variables.

The results show that the neighborhood variables which are most directly related to price changes are those describing the use of neighborhood-based institutions. Neighborhoods that are desirable because of their institutional base—those in which people shop, worship and participate—experience greater rates of price appreciation than those where the institutional base is not as strong.

The social fabric of the neighborhood is not an important contributing factor to the economic appreciation of the neighborhood. In fact, the analysis of short-run price changes shows that many of the neighborhood social support variables are inversely related to price appreciation. Those neighborhoods experiencing the greatest gains in their real estate market are the ones in which the residents are least apt to have relatives, best social friends or providers of emotional support residing there. This is consistent with Chapters 2, 3, 4, and 6 which have shown that these are the neighborhoods in which residents have the greatest choices. It follows that they are the most desirable neighborhoods, and therefore the price appreciation should be the greatest.

The thesis of the community of limited liability explains these results. Because residents of the most desirable locations maintain their support structure outside of the neighborhood, the social fabric of these areas is less strong. Therefore, the economic health of a neighborhood, if it is measured in terms of real estate price changes, will not necessarily reflect the underlying strength of the neighborhood's social structure. The economic health depends on many attributes of the neighborhood and on the relative attractiveness of these attributes compared to alternative locations.

It is also necessary to understand the importance of the institutional structure of the neighborhood, particularly for neighborhoods with income levels less than the city-wide mean. The neighborhoods in that group with the greatest price appreciation are the ones in which residents are more likely to shop, worship, and participate in neighborhood groups and community organizations. As the income level of the neighborhood falls, the residents have less opportunity to participate outside of the neighborhood, and therefore the institutional base of the neighborhood becomes more important. As the institutional base becomes more attractive to current and potential residents, it generates increased demand for living in the neighborhood, and this is picked up directly in terms of a stronger real estate market and greater price appreciation.

CHAPTER 8

The Neighborhood Context

INTRODUCTION

Previous chapters have shown that the characteristics of the respondents, by influencing their choices and constraints, significantly affect the way in which they use the neighborhood and thereby the sense of community that is created. The analysis, however, has been mostly performed at the individual level and has not examined how the contextual (structural) influence of the neighborhood affects its residents' behavior.[1]

This chapter examines the interrelationship between the respondents and the neighborhood in which they live in order to assess the impact of the environmental context on attitudes and behavior. In order to study this relationship, neighborhoods were grouped by their racial composition, and responses to the survey questions were analyzed for similar racial and income groups within each of the neighborhood types.

---

[1]For a discussion of the contextual or structural effects, see Peter M. Blau, "Structural Effects," *American Sociological Review* 25 (April 1960): 178–93; James A. Davis, Joe L. Spaeth, and Carolyn Huson, "A Technique for Analyzing the Effects of Group Composition," *American Sociological Review* 26 (April 1961): 215–25; and William H. Sewell and Michael J. Armer, "Neighborhood Context and College Plans," *American Sociological Review* 31 (April 1966): 159–68.

The contextual effects were isolated by examining responses for similar groups of respondents across the neighborhood classifications. If contextual effects are present, the responses of like groups of individuals should vary as the racial composition of the neighborhood changes.

The multilevel contingency table analysis used in this chapter does not permit all potentially relevant variables to be held constant. Race and income are the only controls being used to ensure uniformity in the characteristics of the respondents among neighborhood groups. Although other variables could also be changing, which could account for the observed differences, nevertheless conclusions are usually consistent for each income group, and therefore there is some assurance that it is the structural influence which is being observed and not the result of uncontrolled differences in the data.

The analysis undertaken in this chapter is based upon the assumption that the racial composition of the neighborhood is a valid parameter for stratification purposes in order to observe contextual effects. Race was selected because it correlated moderately well at the neighborhood level with income (0.59), homeownership (0.34), and ethnicity (as identified by the Catholic population in the neighborhood, 0.80), and because the racial composition of the neighborhood is highly visible and may be expected to have psychological and behavioral implications that other socioeconomic variables would not have.

The racial composition of the neighborhood is also a useful variable on which to stratify neighborhoods because it is a proxy for the choices and constraints facing the residents. Previous chapters have suggested that blacks may not have had equal access to the city's housing stock and neighborhoods. Therefore, part of what is ascribed to the neighborhood context may be a result of differences in the opportunities available to the residents as well as to variations in the community which has been constructed within the neighborhood.

NEIGHBORHOOD CLASSIFICATION

Pittsburgh's neighborhoods were broken down into classifications of white, mixed, and black, based upon their racial characteristics. White neighborhoods are those with a black population of less than 30% of the total (50 neighborhoods); mixed are those with a black population between 30% and 59% of the total (9 neighborhoods); and black neighborhoods are those with a black population of 60% or more (15 neighborhoods). Median household income, average respondent age, and homeownership rates in these neighborhood groups are shown in Table 26 for white and black respondents. Not surprisingly, these statistics vary for each racial group in each type of neighborhood. The sample was further stratified by income group ($0–$10,000; $10,001–$20,000; $20,001 and above). Table 27 lists the number of respondents falling into each of these categories.

AFFECTIVE SENTIMENTS

The analysis in Chapter 3 showed that black respondents were more attached to their neighborhood than whites. This is not true, however, for all types of neighborhoods or for all types of respondents. Table 28 shows that whites living in predominantly white neighborhoods are more attached than blacks living in these neighborhoods, but that most blacks living in mixed or primarily black neighborhoods report greater attachment than whites living in those locations. The table also shows a decrease in the level of attachment as the racial dominance of a given group declines (this does not hold for all income groups in mixed neighborhoods). This applies to both whites and blacks, although the decline is much more significant in the case of white respondents. These conclusions suggest that there may be an interactive effect between the racial

Table 26. Selected Socioeconomic Characteristics of White, Mixed, and Black Neighborhoods

Characteristics	White	Mixed	Black	Total sample
	Neighborhood group			
Median household income	$14,650	$10,450	$8,350	
White respondents	14,830	11,140	9,640	$13,200
Black respondents	12,250	9,820	8,080	
Homeownership rate	66%	50%	56%	
White respondents	68	61	62	63%
Black respondents	43	34	54	
Median age				
White respondents	47.9	47.9	50.9	
Black respondents	40.3	45.2	52.9	48.3

Source: 1980 Citizen Survey.

Table 27. Number of Respondents in Each Neighborhood and Income Group by Race of the Respondent

Neighborhood type and respondent income group	Whites	Blacks
	Number of respondents	
White neighborhoods	3,715	183
$0–$10,000	1,195	75
$10,001–$20,000	1,395	63
$20,001 and above	1,125	45
Racially mixed neighborhoods	278	197
$0–$10,000	128	101
$10,001–$20,000	88	68
$20,001 and above	62	28
Black neighborhoods	164	776
$0–$10,000	85	473
$10,001–$20,000	54	222
$20,001 and above	25	81

Source: 1980 Citizen Survey.

Table 28. Neighborhood Attachment by Racial Characteristics of the Neighborhood and Income and Race of the Respondent

Neighborhood type and respondent income	Strong or very strongly attached (percentage)	
	White respondents	Black respondents
White neighborhoods	66%	55%
$0–$10,000	66	53
$10,001–$20,000	63	57
$20,001 and above	67	57
Racially mixed neighborhoods	51%	57%
$0–$10,000	53	56
$10,001–$20,000	42	60
$20,001 and above	55	43
Black neighborhoods	56%	64%
$0–$10,000	49	64
$10,001–$20,000	43	61
$20,001 and above	60	72

Source: 1980 Citizen Survey.

composition of a neighborhood and the attitudes of its residents. Sense of community is stronger for people in neighborhoods in which they are a majority because they are more likely to interact and participate in neighborhood activities than they would be if they were a minority.

Similar conclusions hold for neighborhood satisfaction. In Chapter 3 whites were shown to be more satisfied with their neighborhood than were blacks, and this is borne out by the results shown in Table 29. In all three types of neighborhoods, higher percentages of whites than blacks rate the neighborhood a good or excellent place to live; however, as the percentage of blacks in the neighborhood rises, the satisfaction level of most whites and blacks declines. Because the satisfaction level of both blacks and whites is lower in black neighborhoods, this may indicate that there is something inherently different in those areas that is directly related to people's attitudes, or that the quality of public services available in those locations does

Table 29. Neighborhood Satisfaction by Racial Characteristics of the Neighborhood and Income and Race of the Respondent

Neighborhood type and respondent income	Rating neighborhood good or excellent (percentage)	
	White respondents	Black respondents
White neighborhoods	81%	67%
$0–$10,000	72	52
$10,001–$20,000	81	76
$20,001 and above	89	77
Racially mixed neighborhoods	56%	53%
$0–$10,000	49	46
$10,001–$20,000	51	56
$20,001 and above	69	64
Black neighborhoods	56%	47%
$0–$10,000	51	46
$10,001–$20,000	54	46
$20,001 and above	80	58

Source: 1980 Citizen Survey.

not match the tastes, preferences, needs, and/or expectations of the residents as well as it does in other locations.

Unfortunately, the research does not provide conclusive evidence on the reasons for the lower satisfaction levels in black neighborhoods. However, it does show that the level of satisfaction with neighborhood public services diminishes as the racial concentration of the neighborhood rises. The following sections discuss in more detail the variations that exist between types of neighborhoods, and this may help to provide additional insight into factors associated with the observed contextual effects.

USE OF NEIGHBORHOOD FACILITIES

The neighborhood context is important in terms of the uses made of the neighborhood for grocery shopping, shopping for small items, and attending religious services.

Whites in white neighborhoods are much more likely to use these facilities in or near their neighborhood than they are if they live in a black neighborhood. Blacks, however, are more inclined to attend religious services in or near their neighborhood if they live in a black rather than in a white or mixed neighborhood. Within each neighborhood type, shopping within the area tends to increase as household income rises. This most likely indicates that within each neighborhood group, those with higher incomes will select the neighborhoods offering the greatest amenities and convenience. There is a mixed tendency with respect to attending church or other religious organizations (see Table 30).

Black neighborhoods have the lowest rates of utilization of all of these services except for the attendance of reli-

Table 30. Use of Facilities in or near the Neighborhood by Racial Characteristics of the Neighborhood and Income and Race of the Respondent

| Neighborhood type and respondent income group | Percentage all or most of the time | | | | | |
| | Main grocery shopping | | Shopping for small items | | Attending religious services | |
	Whites	Blacks	Whites	Blacks	Whites	Blacks
White neighborhoods	68%	68%	49%	40%	57%	33%
$0–$10,000	64	64	45	35	57	25
$10,001–$20,000	67	68	49	40	59	38
$20,001 and above	73	76	56	47	56	33
Racially mixed neighborhoods	64%	65%	41%	41%	45%	31%
$0–$10,000	61	60	40	38	50	29
$10,001–$20,000	66	74	46	46	41	30
$20,001 and above	73	82	36	46	39	32
Black neighborhoods	49%	48%	38%	32%	41%	38%
$0–$10,000	35	48	32	30	42	39
$10,001–$20,000	59	47	42	34	41	36
$20,001 and above	68	54	56	42	36	43

Source: 1980 Citizen Survey.

gious services. However, whites in all neighborhoods attend church in or near their place of residence at higher rates than do blacks in black neighborhoods.

Part of the explanation for the less frequent use of these facilities in black neighborhoods is availability. Twenty-eight percent of the white and 18% of the black respondents living in black neighborhoods report that there is no store available in or near their neighborhood in which they could do their grocery shopping. This compares to the corresponding percentages for whites and blacks living in white neighborhoods of 8% and 10%, respectively. Similar circumstances apply to the availability of small-item stores. However, even when reported availability is controlled for, both whites and blacks make less use of their neighborhood for shopping if they live in a black neighborhood than they do if they live in a white neighborhood. This may indicate that the quality of available shopping facilities is poorer in black neighborhoods. (Religious institutions are equally available within or near to both black and white neighborhoods.) Less availability and poorer quality of the stores located in black neighborhoods help to explain the lower levels of neighborhood satisfaction expressed by respondents in these areas.

NEIGHBORING

Neighboring activities are influenced by the racial composition of the neighborhood for whites but not to a significant extent for blacks. As the neighborhood goes from white to black, borrowing by whites declines from 30% to 18%, visiting from 56% to 39%, and helping from 64% to 49%. Although these three activities occur slightly less often for blacks in black neighborhoods than for blacks in white neighborhoods, the decline is not large as it is for whites (see Table 31).

Whites at all income levels borrow, visit, and help more in white neighborhoods than blacks living in these

*Table 31. Neighboring Activities by Racial Characteristics of the
Neighborhood and Income and Race of the Respondent*

Neighborhood type and respondent income group	Percentage of respondents engaging in the activity often or sometimes					
	Borrowing from neighbors		Visiting with neighbors		Helping or being helped by neighbors	
	White	Black	White	Black	White	Black
White neighborhoods	30%	16%	56%	48%	64%	55%
$0–$10,000	22	12	50	47	58	49
$10,001–$20,000	33	18	58	49	66	57
$20,001 and above	40	18	62	47	70	60
Racially mixed neighborhoods	29%	16%	43%	39%	55%	54%
$0–$10,000	19	18	37	36	48	51
$10,001–$20,000	35	16	44	43	61	57
$20,001 and above	42	14	52	36	64	67
Black neighborhoods	18%	15%	39%	41%	49%	52%
$0–$10,000	20	13	41	40	49	50
$10,001–$20,000	15	19	33	42	46	48
$20,001 and above	24	16	44	46	56	68

Source: 1980 Citizen Survey.

areas. In racially mixed neighborhoods whites borrow to a greater extent and visit slightly more often than blacks; differences in the rate of helping vary depending upon the income group. In black neighborhoods, whites borrow more than blacks at the upper- and lower-income levels, while blacks in almost every income group help and visit to a slightly greater extent than whites. Neighboring activities generally increase with income for whites in all types of neighborhoods. For blacks, helping is the only neighboring activity which is very income-sensitive.

The neighborhood setting influences the extent of neighboring for whites, but not appreciably for blacks. Blacks neighbor slightly less in black neighborhoods than in white neighborhoods, but the fall-off is not large; and compared to whites, blacks neighbor more in black neighborhoods, and only in these locations, than do whites.

SOCIAL SUPPORTS

Social support systems were examined in terms of the place of residence of the person with whom the respondent socializes most frequently, the place of residence of the person the respondent is most likely to call upon to discuss personal concerns, relatives living in the neighborhood, and household composition.

Except for whites living in mixed neighborhoods, there is not a significant change across the neighborhood classifications in the percentage of respondents having their best social friend living in the neighborhood. For both whites and blacks the percentage varies from 53% to 59%. The likelihood, however, varies by income. For whites, as income increases, the respondent is more likely to have the friend living outside of the neighborhood. This is also true for blacks, except in white neighborhoods, in which case lower-income blacks are less likely to have their friend living in the neighborhood. Except in this instance, the relationship between place of residence and income clearly follows the predictions of the choice-constraint model. People are more likely to have ties external to the neighborhood as income rises (see Table 32).

The willingness of respondents to talk over their emotional concerns varies slightly for both whites and blacks as the percentage of black neighborhood residents rises. In going from white to black neighborhoods, there is a decrease in the willingness of respondents to talk over personal concerns; the rate falls from 77% of the white and 79% of the black respondents in white neighborhoods to 68% and 69%, respectively, for whites and blacks living in black neighborhoods. Thus, there is a slight contextual effect operating here. Willingness generally rises with income except for blacks living in white neighborhoods, where the opposite applies.

For the respondents who are willing to talk over their emotional concerns, the location of the individual they are most likely to turn to varies by neighborhood type. Thirty-

Table 32. Place of Residence of Primary Social Friend and Provider of Emotional Supports by Racial Characteristics of the Neighborhood and Income and Race of the Respondent

| Neighborhood type and respondent income group | Percentage of respondents with the contact living in the neighborhood | | | |
| | Social friend | | Provider of emotional supports | |
	Whites	Blacks	Whites	Blacks
White neighborhoods	55%	56%	32%	30%
$0–$10,000	62	53	35	36
$10,001–$20,000	53	57	32	24
$20,001 and above	50	61	29	25
Racially mixed neighborhoods	44%	54%	22%	33%
$0–$10,000	46	59	29	36
$10,001–$20,000	43	52	15	33
$20,001 and above	34	39	22	39
Black neighborhoods	53%	59%	25%	36%
$0–$10,000	62	65	23	38
$10,001–$20,000	50	51	15	28
$20,001 and above	29	49	42	36

Source: 1980 Citizen Survey.

two percent of the white respondents in white areas report that this person lives in their neighborhood, compared to 25% of the whites living in black neighborhoods. Thirty percent of the blacks living in white locations state that this person lives in their neighborhood, compared to 36% of the blacks in black neighborhoods. Therefore, there is a slight contextual influence operating here as well. Respondents who are a minority in a neighborhood are more likely to have their primary provider of emotional supports living outside of the neighborhood than they are when they live in neighborhoods in which they are a majority. Blacks are much more likely than whites to have this person residing in their neighborhood in black or mixed areas but are less likely to when they live in neighborhoods that are predominantly white.

A higher percentage of whites have relatives in the neighborhood if they live in a white as opposed to a black area (45% compared to 34 %). Blacks living in black neighborhoods are more likely to have relatives in the neighborhood than they are if they live in white neighborhoods (46% compared to 35%). There is no clear-cut relationship with respect to income. That is, higher-income respondents are neither more nor less likely to have relatives in the neighborhood.

The composition of the household varies significantly by the characteristics of the neighborhood. A higher percentage of whites living in white neighborhoods are married than is the case for whites living in other locations (59% of the respondents compared to 44% in each of the other two groups of neighborhoods); whites are less likely to be separated or divorced or widowed in white neighborhoods than in other areas (21% compared to 27% in mixed neighborhoods and 32% in black neighborhoods). Blacks living in white neighborhoods are also more likely to be married or single. Blacks living in white neighborhoods are less likely to be separated, divorced, or widowed than they are in the other types of neighborhoods (23% compared to 37% in mixed and 42% in black neighborhoods). The presence of a nuclear family, therefore, decreases as the concentration of the black population rises. Family composition is also related to income. The lowest income group has the highest percentage of separated, divorced, or widowed households, rising from 41% of the whites in this income group in white neighborhoods to 49% in black neighborhoods, and increasing from 37% of the blacks in this income category in white neighborhoods to 56% in black neighborhoods (see Table 33).

Whites and blacks are more likely to have neighborhood supports in those neighborhoods in which they are a majority. Thus it is not surprising that attachment to the neighborhood is highest for people in the places in which they are racially dominant.

Table 33. Household Composition by Racial Characteristics of the
Neighborhood and Income and Race of the Respondent

Neighborhood type and respondent income group	Percentage of white respondents		Percentage of black respondents	
	Married	Separated/ divorced/ widowed	Married	Separated/ divorced/ widowed
White neighborhoods	59%	21%	43%	23%
$0–$10,000	33	41	21	37
$10,001–$20,000	67	13	54	9
$20,001 and above	77	8	58	18
Racially mixed neighborhoods	44%	27%	37%	37%
$0–$10,000	26	44	21	55
$10,001–$20,000	53	14	49	22
$20,001 and above	69	10	57	7
Black neighborhoods	44%	32%	41%	42%
$0–$10,000	28	49	28	56
$10,001–$20,000	57	15	56	24
$20,001 and above	68	8	69	12

Source: 1980 Citizen Survey.

ORGANIZATIONAL INVOLVEMENT

Twenty-two percent of the blacks participate in neighborhood issue organizations in black neighborhoods, compared to 9% if they live in white neighborhoods. Whites' involvement in neighborhood issue organizations is also higher in neighborhoods in which they are a majority (16% in white neighborhoods compared to 13% in black neighborhoods). Therefore, the neighborhood context influences participation, and the influence is particularly evident in the case of blacks. Participation is directly related to income in all neighborhood types. Higher-income respondents belong to organizations concerned about neighborhood problems more frequently than do lower-income households (see Table 34).

Membership in other voluntary organizations also var-

Table 34. *Organizational Involvement by Racial Characteristics of the Neighborhood and Income and Race of the Respondent*

Neighborhood type and respondent income group	Percentage of respondents who belong to neighborhood issue organization		Percentage of respondents who belong to other voluntary organizations (in /near neighborhood)	
	Whites	Blacks	Whites	Blacks
White neighborhoods	16%	9%	56% (36%)	51% (27%)
$0–$10,000	13	5	48 (34)	37 (19)
$10,001–$20,000	14	15	56 (36)	56 (33)
$20,001 and above	23	9	65 (40)	67 (31)
Racially mixed neighborhoods	16%	20%	49% (27%)	57% (34%)
$0–$10,000	13	20	38 (26)	53 (33)
$10,001–$20,000	5	18	57 (25)	54 (32)
$20,001 and above	32	29	61 (31)	79 (36)
Black neighborhoods	13%	22%	43% (22%)	58% (35%)
$0–10,000	11	19	38 (24)	53 (35)
$10,001–$20,000	11	24	48 (24)	60 (35)
$20,001 and above	21	31	56 (16)	80 (36)

Source: 1980 Citizen Survey.

ies by neighborhood group. Whites participate to the greatest extent in white neighborhoods and blacks belong at higher rates in black neighborhoods. Higher-income respondents participate at higher rates than lower-income persons. The percentage of those other organizations located in or near the neighborhood declines for whites as the racial composition of the neighborhood rises. In the case of blacks, however, the rate remains relatively constant for most income groups (see Table 34).

Membership in voluntary organizations varies across the different types of neighborhoods, and the change in the participation rate is particularly evident in the case of blacks. Therefore, the racial context of the neighborhood has an effect on the participatory behavior of the residents. Since participation is one way to bring people together to support and create a sense of community, it makes sense that people's attachments to their neighborhood are highest in the locations in which participation occurs most frequently.

LIFE HAPPINESS

Neighborhood type is also related to the respondent's life happiness. Both whites and blacks are happier in white neighborhoods than they are in black neighborhoods. Higher-income respondents are generally happier than those with less income. There were no significant contextual effects associated with responses to the life satisfaction survey question (see Table 35).

DISCUSSION

Neighborhoods differ along a number of dimensions. These include the institutional base of the neighborhood; social fabric; friendliness and industriousness of neighbors; quality of life; location relative to job, cultural activities, and shopping; and race, ethnicity, and income, which account for some of the variations in culture and class. Undoubtedly, differences in these characteristics will influence the way people feel about the neighborhood and their attachment and commitment toward it.

The discussions in prior chapters have shown that people's affective sentiments toward the neighborhood are related to a number of these variables. The analysis undertaken in this chapter, building upon the earlier work, attempted to ascertain whether the structural or contextual aspects of the neighborhood had an effect upon people's attitudes and behavior. The results suggest that contextual effects are present. Whites express greater attachment to and satisfaction with their neighborhood in predominantly white neighborhoods than they do in predominantly black

Table 35. Life Happiness by Racial Characteristics of the Neighborhood and Income and Race of the Respondent

Neighborhood type and respondent income group	Percentage of respondents not happy with life	
	Whites	Blacks
White neighborhoods	15%	20%
$0–$10,000	20	23
$10,001–$20,000	12	18
$20,001 and above	10	21
Racially mixed neighborhoods	23%	22%
$0–$10,000	30	25
$10,001–$20,000	22	21
$20,001 and above	12	14
Black neighborhoods	31%	30%
$0–$10,000	34	33
$10,001–$20,000	32	26
$20,001 and above	20	26

Source: 1980 Citizen Survey.

neighborhoods. Whites participate in neighboring activities to a greater extent in white neighborhoods. Whites are more apt to talk over personal problems in white neighborhoods, and when they do, there is a greater likelihood that they will turn to somebody living in their neighborhood if most of their neighbors are white. Whites in white areas are more likely to have relatives living there than if they live in neighborhoods of other racial composition. Whites are more likely to shop and attend religious services in or near their place of residence if they live in a white neighborhood. Finally, whites are slightly more likely to belong to a neighborhood organization and other voluntary groups if they live in white as compared to black neighborhoods. These conclusions generally hold for all income groups; therefore, these differences cannot be explained by variations in the income levels of the respondents across the three types of neighborhoods.

These results show that whites living in neighborhoods in which they are the dominant group are more positive about their place of residence, have stronger neighborhood support systems, and are more likely to neighbor, to use neighborhood facilities, and to participate in neighborhood organizations than are whites living elsewhere. As a result, it is not surprising to observe that whites living in white neighborhoods report greater life happiness than whites residing in racially mixed or black areas.

The conclusions for black respondents are not so crystal clear as those for whites. Blacks are more attached to their neighborhood if they live in a predominantly black neighborhood than if they live in other locations; however, blacks are more satisfied with the neighborhood if they live in a white neighborhood. The neighborhood context does not seem to affect neighboring patterns for blacks. Blacks are less likely to talk over emotional concerns as the percentage of blacks within the neighborhood rises, but when they do they are more likely to turn to somebody in their own neighborhood if they reside in a predominantly black area. Blacks living in black neighborhoods are also more likely to participate in organizations concerned about neighborhood issues as well as other types of voluntary organizations. Finally, blacks in black neighborhoods are less likely to shop there but are more likely to attend church there and participate in neighborhood organizations than they are if they live in a white area. Blacks living in white locations are happier with their life than blacks living in black neighborhoods.

It is obvious from the analysis that, for white respondents, white neighborhoods are much more supportive of positive sentiments and interpersonal relationships than are black neighborhoods. Black neighborhoods, however, do not necessarily provide a more supportive environment for their black residents. Black respondents report more positive attitudes about life and greater neighborhood satisfaction in white neighborhoods than they do in black areas. The reasons for this are not apparent. It could be that the quality of life, of public services, and of the institutions serving white neighborhoods is superior to those serving black neighborhoods. This could be part of the answer, but it is most likely not all of it. There is a distinct difference in the composition of households for all groups living in black compared to white neighborhoods. White and black respondents are more likely to be married in white neighborhoods, although the percentage difference for blacks living in white and black neighborhoods is small; and there is a significant increase in the percentage of separated, divorced, and widowed households living in black neighborhoods for both races. This applies to all income groups, and the rate is significantly higher for blacks than it is for whites. Forty-two percent of the black respondents do not live in a nuclear family in black neighborhoods, and therefore the supports provided by a spouse are not available for a large percentage of this population group. This difference, coupled with the fact that the median age of black respondents living in black neighborhoods is the highest of any group, may be part of the explanation for what has been referred to as the contextual effect of black neighborhoods.

The findings show that attachment to place of residence is influenced by the social fabric of the neighborhood. Sense of community is strongest in those neighborhoods where people have the strongest communal bonds. These are places of greater racial homogeneity in which interaction among the residents is shown to be higher. Neighborhoods in which people are more similar tend to foster a stronger sense of community because one potential barrier to interaction—race—is removed.

Satisfaction with place is determined by the physical characteristics of the neighborhood. It is higher for blacks in white neighborhoods, in part, because these neighborhoods offer greater convenience for shopping. The higher satisfaction levels shown by whites may reflect the greater choice they have in selecting a place to live. Whites have greater median household incomes than blacks in every neighborhood type, and therefore they have more opportunity to choose a neighborhood which offers them the type of personal interaction and physical amenities they desire.

The choices and constraints that people face influence their sentiments toward their neighborhood and to their life as a whole. Whites in white neighborhoods have the greatest choice and are able to select the neighborhoods that offer them preferred amenities, services, and social contacts; hence they express higher levels of attachment and satisfaction than whites in other locations. Their greater life happiness is entirely consistent with this result.

Blacks in black neighborhoods, on the other hand, have fewer choices than many of the blacks living in other neighborhood types, and therefore their lower levels of neighborhood satisfaction reflect their limited opportunities to find a neighborhood which best meets their needs. The higher level of attachment shown by blacks living in black neighborhoods compared to blacks elsewhere, however, may not be a result of the same positive influence as it is for whites in white neighborhoods. These whites are attracted to a neighborhood because of the positive rewards and gratifications it offers, whereas the blacks in black neighborhoods are attracted not only because of the social fabric but also out of necessity because their other options are few. This interpretation is consistent with the lower levels of life happiness expressed by blacks in black neighborhoods compared to their counterparts living in more racially mixed neighborhoods. The slightly stronger social fabric for blacks in black neighborhoods does not provide strong enough supports to offset the higher life stresses felt by those individuals; and some of this stress is a result of the fewer choices they have to resolve problems and meet needs.

CHAPTER 9

The Implications of Income

INTRODUCTION

Chapter 8 showed that people's attitudes toward their neighborhood are associated with its racial composition and that this in turn is related to the choices and constraints facing the residents. However, given that neighborhoods will vary along a number of characteristics, a more detailed examination of individual neighborhoods is required in order to obtain a better understanding of which characteristics or combinations thereof are associated with more positive feelings of attachment and satisfaction. This additional analysis will provide a better perspective for assessing the interrelationships among a number of variables, thus depicting the contextual characteristics of neighborhoods which are associated with a stronger social fabric.

In this chapter neighborhoods are stratified on the basis of their income. Income was selected as the basis for stratification because previous analysis has shown that the economic level of the neighborhood is an important explanatory variable for differences among neighborhoods in terms of the composition of the social fabric and the feelings that people have about their place of residence.

The income groups were constructed from the standardized value of each neighborhood's mean household income as determined from the 1980 citizen survey. Neighborhoods were categorized into the following groups depending upon their relationship to the city's mean household income:

- *High income.* Neighborhoods with income more than one standard deviation above the city-wide mean (12 neighborhoods)
- *Middle income.* Neighborhoods with income up to one standard deviation above the city-wide mean (23 neighborhoods)
- *Moderate income.* Neighborhoods with income less than the city-wide mean by up to one standard deviation (28 neighborhoods)
- *Low income.* Neighborhoods with income less than the city-wide mean by more than one standard deviation (11 neighborhoods)

Each of the groups is described in the following sections.

HIGH-INCOME NEIGHBORHOODS

Twelve neighborhoods have income which exceed the city mean by at least one standard deviation. These neighborhoods have levels of resident satisfaction and neighboring which equal or exceed the city mean for these variables in all cases. The attachment of residents to the neighborhoods in this group does not vary from the average rate for the city, but five of the neighborhoods have levels above and seven have levels below the city-wide rate. Use of neighborhood facilities for shopping and worship is slightly lower than the city average, but use varies among the twelve neighborhoods with four being above and eight below the city mean. (See Table 36 for summary statistics for the four neighborhood groups; Table 37 contains statistics for each neighborhood in the high-income subgroup.)

Compared to the rest of the city, primary ties are more likely to be external for the neighborhoods in this group. Ten neighborhoods have a lower percentage of residents with relatives in the neighborhood, seven have lower per-

Table 36. Selected Statistics for High-, Middle-, Moderate-, and Low-Income Neighborhood Groups[a]

Neighborhood group (number of neighbor-hoods)	Percentage living in neighborhood			Neighbor-hood boring[b]	Use of neighbor-hood facilities[c]	Percentage attached to neighbor-hood[d]	Percentage satisfied with neighbor-hood[e]	Average number of years in neighbor-hood	Percentage of home-ownership	Percentage of blacks/Catholics/Jews
	Relatives	Best friend	Provider of emotional support							
High-income (12)	36%	51%	28%	83	117	63%	89%	17	67%	5% (B)
Middle-income (23)	44	53	31	82	122	65	81	20	70	6 (B)
Moderate-income (28)	49	57	35	76	118	63	61	24	60	34 (B)
Low-income (11)	41	60	30	71	113	60	45	22	39	71 (B)

[a]The high-income group includes all neighborhoods with mean household income at least one standard deviation above the city mean; the middle-income group includes all neighborhoods with mean household income up to one standard deviation above the city mean; the moderate-income group includes all neighborhoods with mean household income up to one standard deviation below the city mean; and the low-income group includes all neighborhoods with mean household income more than one standard deviation below the city mean.

[b]The figure shown is the value of the neighboring index for each neighborhood. The index was constructed by summing and weighting equally answers to the following four survey questions: frequency of borrowing or exchanging things with neighbors, frequency of visiting neighbors, frequency of helping (or being helped by) neighbors with small tasks, and willingness to call on neighbors for help in an emergency. The borrowing, visiting, and helping questions were coded on a 4-point scale, with higher values showing more frequent neighboring; the emergency question was coded Yes = 1; No = 0. The value of the actual index for each neighborhood was multiplied by 10; therefore, the maximum value is 130.

[c]The figure shown is the value of the neighborhood facilities use index for each neighborhood. The index was constructed by summing and weighting equally answers to the survey questions which asked the respondents how often they did the following in or near their neighborhood: main grocery shopping, shopping for small items, attending church or other religious organizations, using health facilities or medical services, and engaging in recreation activities. The questions were coded on a 4-point scale, with higher values showing more frequent use in or near the neighborhood. The value of the actual index for each neighborhood was multiplied by 10; therefore, the maximum value is 200.

[d]Percentage of respondents strongly or very strongly attached to the neighborhood.

[e]Percentage of respondents rating the neighborhood a good or excellent place to live.

Table 37. High-Income Neighborhoods: Selected Statistics[a]

Neighborhood	Percentage living in neighborhood			Neighboring[b]	Use of neighborhood facilities[c]	Percentage attached to neighborhood[d]	Percentage satisfied with neighborhood[e]	Average number of years in neighborhood	Percentage of home-ownership	Percentage of blacks/Catholics/Jews
	Relatives	Best social friend	Provider of emotional support							
Harpen Hilltop–Ridgemont	30%	42%	6%	94	114	69%	82%	19	95%	52%(C)
Chicken Hill	37	40	20	86	118	56	84	17	81	50 (C)
East Carnegie	41	66	36	88	108	33	75	20	66	66 (C)
Banksville	30	55	14	86	123	59	91	17	86	56 (C)
Stanton Heights	37	48	23	88	106	69	91	18	88	59 (C)
Morningside	37	58	28	86	125	62	88	21	76	72 (C)
Highland Park	35	41	25	81	112	60	83	17	56	38 (C)
Squirrel Hill-North	33	52	35	83	116	64	92	16	66	34 (J)
Squirrel Hill-South	45	57	33	79	128	65	92	17	53	55 (J)
Point Breeze	16	36	18	80	105	50	81	9	47	38 (B)
Regent Square	6	46	16	87	122	93	93	15	80	60 (C)
Swisshelm Park	75	60	41	87	101	60	95	30	95	52 (C)
Total group	36	51	28	83	117	63	89	17	67	5 (B)
Total city	44	55	32	79	119	63	72	21	63	22 (B)

[a]This group includes all neighborhoods with mean household income at least one standard deviation above the city mean.
[b]The figure shown is the value of the neighboring index for each neighborhood. See footnote b of Table 36 for explanation.
[c]The figure shown is the value of the neighborhood facilities use index for each neighborhood. See footnote c Table 36 for explanation.
[d]Percentage of respondents strongly or very strongly attached to the neighborhood.
[e]Percentage of respondents rating the neighborhood a good or excellent place to live.

centages of best social friend living in the neighborhood, and eight have rates of provider of social supports living in the neighborhood below that for the city as a whole.

The greatest amount of neighboring occurs in these neighborhoods. Sixty-two percent of the respondents in the lowest-income neighborhood group report that they never borrow small items from their neighbors compared to 35% in the highest-income group; 31% in the poorest areas never visit with their neighbors compared to 16% in the richest; and 31% in the lowest-income category state that they never help or are helped by their neighbors as opposed to 19% in the highest-income location (see Table 38).

Membership in organizations concerned about neighborhood issues occurs at slightly higher rates in higher-income neighborhoods (21%, as opposed to 17% in the

Table 38. Neighboring Activities by Income Group

Neighborhood groups ranked on the basis of income (number of neighborhoods)[a]	Percentage of respondents in each income category		
	Who never borrow from neighbors[b]	Who never visit with neighbors[c]	Who never help or are helped by neighbors[d]
High-income (12)	35%	16%	19%
Middle-income (23)	40	17	18
Moderate-income (28)	54	26	26
Low-income (11)	62	31	31

[a]The neighborhood groups were determined on the basis of mean household income. The high-income group includes all neighborhoods with mean household income at least one standard deviation above the city mean; middle-income includes neighborhoods with mean household income up to one standard deviation above the city mean; moderate-income includes those with mean household income less than one standard deviation below the city mean; and low-income consists of those with mean household income more than one standard deviation under the city mean.
[b]The survey question was, "How often do you borrow or exchange things with your neighbors?" Response categories: often, sometimes, rarely or never.
[c]The survey question was, "How often do you visit with your neighbors?" Same response categories as above.
[d]The survey question was, "Within the past year, how often have people in this neighborhood helped you or you helped them with small tasks, such as repair work or grocery shopping?" Same response categories as above.

lower-income group). Similarly, participation in other types of voluntary organizations occurs more often in or near the neighborhood in the higher-income group than it does in the others (38%, versus 30% in the lowest-income group).

General life happiness is found to be directly related to the income level of the neighborhood. Twenty-eight percent of those in the high-income neighborhoods report that they are very happy with their life, compared to 19% in the low-income group; conversely, only 10% of those in the higher-income category state that they are not too happy, compared to 32% in the lowest-income group.

Life satisfaction shows a similar relationship. Thirty-three percent of those in the top-income group are very satisfied with their life as a whole, as opposed to 19% in the bottom-income category.

The higher-income neighborhoods are primarily homeowner. Only three have homeownership rates less than that for the city as a whole. The tenure of residents is generally less than in other neighborhoods. Respondents in all but two of these areas have resided there shorter periods of time, on the average, than is the norm for the city as a whole.

Pittsburgh's higher-income neighborhoods are good examples of the liberated neighborhood—the community of limited liability. Participation in neighborhood organizations and neighboring—the maintenance of secondary relationships among residents—are high, yet there is a pull from outside of the neighborhood from the sources of the resident's primary ties. The effect of these push–pull relationships on the affective sentiments toward the neighborhood is observed in terms of high resident satisfaction and levels of attachment which are not appreciably different from the city-wide mean. Higher satisfaction makes sense because these residents have the greatest economic choice of where to live and can select that location which best meets their needs. It is more difficult to predict neighborhood attachment. Neighboring would be expected to strengthen it, but the outward orientation with respect to location of family and friends would be expected to weaken the communal bonds in these locations.

Discussion

Most of the neighborhoods in this group have similar response patterns, with the exception of Squirrel Hill South of Forbes and Swisshelm Park. These two areas have stronger primary ties in the neighborhood than do the others. In Squirrel Hill's case, this may be related to the unique ethnic nature of the neighborhood—55% of the residents are Jewish, the highest percentage of any neighborhood in the city and greatly exceeding that for the city as a whole (6%). (It is interesting to note that some of the highest rates of participation in voluntary organizations in or near the neighborhood occur in the two Squirrel Hill neighborhoods, and that Squirrel Hill North of Forbes has the second highest percentage of Jewish population in the city, approximately 34%.) The greater incidence of neighborhood primary ties in Swisshelm Park may be attributed to the fact that the residents of that neighborhood have lived there longer than have residents of other neighborhoods, and they have lived there much longer than the city mean (30 versus 21 years) (see Table 37).

These examples illustrate why it is not possible to generalize with respect to the social fabric on the basis of a single characteristic of the neighborhood. Differences in the ethnic composition of the neighborhoods and in the tenure of the residents may produce a fabric of social life different from the rest of the neighborhoods in the group. Point Breeze makes this clear as well. This neighborhood is one into which a large percentage of black and white professionals are moving. The average length of time lived in the neighborhood is less than in any other neighborhood in this group, primary ties in the neighborhood are among the weakest, homeownership is the lowest, and neighborhood attachment is the lowest. The internal dynamics of this neighborhood differ from the rest of the neighborhoods in this group, and the strength of the social fabric may be less strong than in other locations where population turn-over is less, homeownership greater, and the social composition more homogeneous. However, the neighborhood is in high demand as a residential community because of its proximity to universities and colleges, its current lower real estate values, and its convenience to shopping and public transportation; and therefore, many of the descriptive characteristics of the neighborhood and its social characteristics give a misleading impression as to its underlying strengths.

MIDDLE-INCOME NEIGHBORHOODS

Twenty-three neighborhoods fall into this category (mean income up to one standard deviation above the city mean). Compared to the higher-income neighborhoods, those in this group have longer resident tenure (15 neighborhoods have values equal to or exceeding the city mean of 21 years); homeownership is slightly higher (but 5 neighborhoods have rates below that for the city); attachment levels are of the same order of magnitude (12 neighborhoods are above and 11 below the city average); and neighborhood satisfaction is slightly lower (7 neighborhoods fall below the city average). (Table 39 contains statistics for each neighborhood in the middle-income subgroup.)

The neighborhoods in this group are beginning to show changes in the social fabric components relative to those in the higher-income group. Neighboring is below the city average in six locations but is more or less comparable to that in the higher-income group. Relatives live in the neighborhood at rates equal to or higher than the city average in 14 locations; best social friend lives in the neighborhood at a rate greater than that for the city in six cases; and provider of emotional support lives in the neighborhood more frequently than the city average in 12 neighborhoods. For all of these variables, primary ties are more prevalent in the middle-income neighborhoods than they are in the upper-income group.

The length of time lived in the neighborhood is associated with the location of primary ties. Of the 15 neighborhoods with resident tenure equal to or above the city mean, 13 have a greater incidence of relatives in the neighborhood, 5 are more likely to have best social friend in the neighborhood (out of 6 for the group as a whole), and 11 have a rate of provider of social supports in the neighborhood equal to or above the city average (out of 12 for the entire group). Primary ties in the neighborhood are also associated directly with the homeownership rate. Neighborhood primary ties are not as strong in any of the locations having homeownership rates below the city average.

In order for one to examine these relationships from a slightly different perspective, neighborhoods were classified as having either strong or weak primary ties on the basis of whether or not the percentages of respondents with relatives, best social friend, or provider of emotional supports living in the neighborhood exceeded the city average. If at least two out of three of these variables had a rate greater than the city average, the neighborhood was classified as having strong primary ties; if only one or none of these variables exceeded the city average, the neighborhood was grouped in the weak primary-ties category. The principal differences between these two groups are seen in the homeownership rates and average length of time lived in the neighborhood. The homeownership rate in the strong-tie neighborhood group is 82%, compared to 58% in the weak-tie group. The average tenure in the strong-tie classification is 24 years as opposed to 17 years in the other group. The strong-tie group also has a slightly larger Catholic population (65% versus 53%), and its residents are slightly more attached to the neighborhood (68% strongly attached versus 61%). There are neither significant differences in the participation rates between these two groups nor in the levels of life happiness or life satisfaction.

Table 39. Middle-Income Neighborhoods: Selected Statistics[a]

| Neighborhood | Percentage living in neighborhood | | | Neighboring[b] | Use of neighborhood facilities[c] | Percentage attached to neighborhood[d] | Percentage satisfied with neighborhood[e] | Average number of years in neighborhood | Percentage of home-ownership | Percentage of blacks/Catholics/Jews |
	Relatives	Best social friend	Provider of emotional support							
Allegheny Center	29%	33%	16%	73	130	35%	71%	11	12%	32%(C)
Spring Hill	54	63	33	83	109	70	73	24	80	54 (C)
Perry North	45	48	29	79	115	60	70	24	77	59 (C)
Brighton Heights	52	49	33	80	130	72	86	25	86	68 (C)
Sheriden-Chartiers	52	54	29	84	119	65	87	23	84	57 (C)
Elliott-West End Valley	44	60	20	86	100	61	70	27	81	80 (C)
Broadhead-Fording	34	40	24	76	106	40	55	14	48	33 (B)
Crafton Heights-Westwood-Oakwood	38	50	25	82	120	61	86	18	83	63 (C)

Mt. Washington-Duquesne Heights	59	61	38	86	126	72	87	23	76	66 (C)
Beechview	41	49	25	84	119	62	83	18	80	73 (C)
Brookline	50	51	33	87	124	57	86	21	86	74 (C)
South Side Slopes	66	54	36	82	129	70	78	30	84	84 (C)
Beltzhoover	52	57	38	72	111	57	49	20	82	60 (B)
Bon Air	55	43	16	76	111	66	95	23	95	44 (C)
Knoxville	48	50	37	80	120	51	61	21	83	65 (C)
Carrick	42	52	33	89	131	67	82	23	78	76 (C)
East Brookline-Overbrook	34	50	38	88	121	69	89	21	88	67 (C)
Lawrenceville-Upper	61	59	45	83	133	81	81	31	81	81 (C)
Shadyside	23	49	27	81	124	65	89	12	32	35 (C)
Friendship	25	51	18	74	129	59	67	9	43	20 (B)
Greenfield	54	61	44	84	127	72	87	22	76	59 (C)
Oakland-North	19	53	21	76	133	53	74	11	28	33 (C)
31st Ward	52	50	32	88	107	70	74	24	87	63 (C)
Total group	44	53	31	82	122	65	81	20	70	6 (B)
Total city	44	55	32	79	119	63	72	21	63	22 (B)

aThis group includes all neighborhoods with mean household income up to one standard deviation above the city mean.

bThe figure shown is the value of the neighboring index for each neighborhood. See footnote *b* of Table 36 for explanation.

cThe figure shown is the value of the neighborhood facilities use index for each neighborhood. See footnote *c* of Table 36 for explanation.

dPercentage of respondents strongly or very strongly attached to the neighborhood.

ePercentage of respondents rating the neighborhood a good or excellent place to live.

Discussion

Within the middle-income group, resident tenure and homeownership are associated with the level of neighboring. Four of the six neighborhoods with neighboring rates less than the city average have a greater percentage of renters than the city as a whole, and all four of these neighborhoods have residents who have lived there, on the average, less than the city mean for neighborhood longevity.

As the income level falls from the high-income group to the middle-income group, other changes are occurring within the neighborhoods as well. Primary ties are becoming more prevalent within the neighborhoods, resident tenure is beginning to increase, and neighborhood satisfaction is starting to decline.

The neighborhoods within this group that are the least strong along a number of different dimensions are those with the highest renter populations. Residents have lived in the five neighborhoods with homeownership rates less than the city average for significantly shorter periods of time than in the other locations (i.e., turnover rates in these neighborhoods are higher); all but one have attachment levels less than the city average; four have neighboring rates lower than the rest of the city; and they all have primary ties that are external to the neighborhood much more frequently than most of the other neighborhoods in this group. These conclusions do not necessarily mean that these neighborhoods are in any kind of difficulty. They merely point out the fact that variables such as tenure and homeownership—factors which tend to pull the resident into the neighborhood—relate directly to the social fabric and sense of community within the neighborhoods in this group. Higher rates of population turnover and low homeownership levels are associated with a social fabric that is weaker than it is in neighborhoods having the opposite characteristics.

Attachment to the neighborhood is associated with the strength of primary ties in the neighborhood. In general, attachment is higher in the neighborhoods in which the residents have stronger ties. This is entirely consistent with Chapters 3 and 6.

MODERATE-INCOME NEIGHBORHOODS

Twenty-eight neighborhoods have a median household income up to one standard deviation less than that for the city as a whole. Residents of these neighborhoods are more likely to have lived there longer than the city average (20 neighborhoods exceed 21 years); homeownership rates are lower here than in the other two groups (14 neighborhoods are above and 14 below the city average); and more neighborhoods have attachment levels above the city average than below it (16 above, 12 below), but the level of attachment for this group, as a whole, is about the same as for the other two groups. Most (21 neighborhoods) report resident satisfaction which is below the city average, and the satisfaction level for the entire group is much less than for the two higher-income categories; and neighboring activities occur less frequently here than in the other two income groups (18 neighborhoods have rates below the city-wide average). Primary ties in the majority of these neighborhoods are more likely to occur within the neighborhood than in the other two groups (residents in 18 neighborhoods are more likely to have relatives residing there; in 16 neighborhoods they are more likely to have their best social friend; and in 16 they are more likely to have their provider of emotional supports living there). (Table 40 contains statistics for each neighborhood in the moderate income subgroup.)

In order for one to obtain additional insights into the differences among neighborhoods in this income group, the 28 neighborhoods were broken down into groups on the basis of race and the strength of the primary ties within the neighborhood, using the procedure described in the previous section. Neighborhoods were considered to have

Table 40. Moderate-Income Neighborhoods: Selected Statistics[a]

Neighborhood	Percentage living in neighborhood			Neighboring[b]	Use of neighborhood facilities[c]	Percentage attached to neighborhood[d]	Percentage satisfied with neighborhood[e]	Average number of years in neighborhood	Percentage of home-ownership	Percentage of blacks/Catholics/Jews
	Relatives	Best social friend	Provider of emotional support							
Manchester	51%	61%	42%	80	110	66%	52%	24	60%	62% (B)
California Avenue	33	50	18	67	98	40	53	23	80	33 (B)
Allegheny West	33	41	11	80	135	83	58	22	66	50 (C)
Central North Side	46	50	23	74	122	66	55	22	52	53 (B)
East North Side	53	66	31	70	134	72	57	29	51	60 (C)
Troy Hill	61	58	32	81	126	68	75	28	61	66 (C)
Perry South	37	53	23	74	106	48	52	24	61	42 (C)
Shadeland-Halls Grove	67	57	48	81	124	61	67	29	76	80 (C)
Esplen	41	41	16	98	123	83	66	27	66	27 (B)
South Side Flats	54	58	37	74	143	77	79	36	65	78 (C)
Arlington	66	71	47	85	116	64	66	25	73	64 (C)
St. Clair	54	53	29	73	98	44	39	24	56	29 (B)
Allentown	67	60	42	78	109	59	65	28	70	78 (C)
Central Business District	10	46	18	73	118	56	75	10	12	33 (C)

Lawrenceville-Lower	57	60	34	85	151	63	61	29	55	74 (C)
Lawrenceville	67	70	41	82	146	77	83	33	66	88 (C)
Garfield	44	48	27	72	117	56	53	19	62	43 (B)
East Liberty	31	47	31	74	119	45	60	11	15	40 (B)
Larimer	35	43	35	69	111	48	35	18	58	77 (B)
Polish Hill	58	67	48	89	127	71	80	25	41	77 (C)
Bloomfield	52	57	42	77	139	66	79	22	49	69 (C)
Homewood North	53	57	34	71	100	58	45	20	71	90 (B)
Homewood South	47	57	33	70	97	55	35	18	46	88 (B)
Lincoln-Lemington-Belmar	33	51	25	72	90	68	57	20	76	76 (B)
East Hills	33	52	26	72	100	57	64	14	73	73 (B)
Oakland South	48	56	35	76	131	78	67	27	72	65 (C)
Hill District-Upper	37	63	46	78	109	77	79	26	70	76 (B)
Hazelwood-Glenwood-Glen Hazel	59	70	49	86	113	66	64	33	68	59 (C)
Total group	49	57	35	76	118	63	61	24	60	34 (B)
Total city	44	55	32	79	119	63	72	21	63	22 (B)

[a] This group includes all neighborhoods with mean household income up to one standard deviation below the city mean.
[b] The figure shown is the value of the neighboring index for each neighborhood. See footnote *b* of Table 36 for explanation.
[c] The figure shown is the value of the neighborhood facilities use index for each neighborhood. See footnote *c* of Table 36 for explanation.
[d] Percentage of respondents strongly or very strongly attached to the neighborhood.
[e] Percentage of respondents rating the neighborhood a good or excellent place to live.

strong primary ties if the values of the variables for relatives, best social friend, and provider of emotional supports
living in the neighborhood were all greater than the city
average. Neighborhoods with weak ties were those in
which these three variables had values less than the city
average. In the few cases in which the pattern was not uniform, neighborhoods were classified strong or weak if two
of the variables had values greater or less than the city
average. The racial breakdown of the neighborhoods was
based upon the criteria used in Chapter 8. Neighborhoods
were classified white, mixed, or black, respectively, if the
black percentage was less than 30%, 30%–59%, or 60%
and above.

Five neighborhood subgroups were identified. Of the
17 white neighborhoods, 12 were classified in the strong-
tie category, and 5 in the weak-tie subgroup. Four neighborhoods were mixed and all of them were classified as
having weak ties. The remaining 7 neighborhoods were
classified black, 4 with strong ties and 3 with weak primary
ties. The neighborhood subgroups were analyzed with
respect to the ten variables shown in Table 40, and the
results are presented in Table 41.

Primary Ties

Primary ties are much stronger in the strong-tie neighborhoods. In the white neighborhoods with strong (weak)
primary ties, 59% (36%) of the respondents have relatives
living in the neighborhood, 63% (51%) have best social
friend, and 40% (23%) have their primary provider of emotional supports. This compares to rates of 49% (35%), 59%
(48%), and 38% (29%), respectively, for relatives, best
social friend, and provider of emotional supports living in
strong-tie or weak-tie black neighborhoods.

Greater primary bonds exist within the strong-tie,
white neighborhoods than in the black or mixed sub-

Table 41. Selected Statistics for Moderate-Income Neighborhoods Stratified by Racial Composition and Strength of Primary Ties[a]

Neighborhood group (number of neighborhoods)	Percentage living in neighborhood			Neighboring[b]	Use of neighborhood facilities[c]	Percentage attached to neighborhood[d]	Percentage satisfied with neighborhood[e]	Average number of years in neighborhood	Percentage of home-ownership	Percentage of blacks/Catholics/Jews
	Relatives	Best social friend	Provider of emotional support							
White neighborhoods										
Strong primary ties (12)	59%	63%	40%	80	130	69%	72%	29	62%	72% (C)
Weak primary ties (5)	36	51	23	75	109	52	55	22	52	43 (C)
Mixed neighborhoods										
Weak primary ties (4)	42	49	26	73	119	57	56	19	50	46 (B)
Black neighborhoods										
Strong primary ties (4)	49	59	38	75	104	62	50	21	62	83 (B)
Weak primary ties (3)	35	48	29	71	101	58	51	18	68	76 (B)

[a]Neighborhoods were classified white, mixed, or black, respectively, if the black percentage was less than 30%, 30–59%, or 60% and above. Neighborhoods were classified as having strong (weak) primary ties if at least two of the three variables for relatives, best social friend, and provider of emotional supports had values greater (less) than the city average.
[b]The figure shown is the value of the neighboring index for each neighborhood. See footnote b of Table 36 for explanation.
[c]The figure shown is the value of the neighborhood facilities use index for each neighborhood. See footnote c of Table 36 for explanation.
[d]Percentage of respondents strongly or very strongly attached to the neighborhood.
[e]Percentage of respondents rating the neighborhood a good or excellent place to live.

groups. The ties in the weak neighborhoods are more or less comparable across the three subgroups.

Affective Sentiments

In the white neighborhoods in which primary bonds are more prevalent, 69% of the residents are strongly attached and 72% rate the neighborhood a good or excellent place to live, compared to 52% and 55%, respectively, in the weak-tie areas. In the black neighborhoods, attachment levels are slightly higher in those areas where primary ties are greater (62% versus 58% in the weak-tie subgroup), and satisfaction levels are about the same irrespective of strength of tie (approximately 50% rate the neighborhood good or excellent in both cases). In the mixed neighborhoods, 57% are strongly attached and 56% give the neighborhood a good or excellent rating (all of the mixed neighborhoods have weak primary ties).

Affective sentiments are much higher in the white neighborhoods having stronger primary ties. Attachment is higher in the strong-tie, black neighborhoods than in all of the weak-tie subgroups, and satisfaction levels are approximately the same among the black, mixed, and white weak-tie subgroups.

Neighboring

The level of neighboring which occurs is slightly higher in the subgroups in which primary ties are more prevalent. In the white (black) neighborhoods, 63% (53%) help their neighbors with small tasks often or sometimes when primary ties are strong, compared to 54% (45%) when ties are weak. Similarly, visiting between neighbors occurs with greater frequency in neighborhoods where interpersonal relationships are the strongest as opposed to in the weaker-tie locations (54% versus 47% in white neighborhoods; 48% versus 39% in black neighborhoods).

Participation

Participation in organizations concerned with neighborhood issues occurs at a slightly higher rate in white neighborhoods having a greater incidence of primary ties (14% versus 11% in the subgroups in which primary ties are less prevalent), and at a much more significant level in black neighborhoods in which primary bonds are more extensive (26% compared to 12% in the weak-tie locations). Participation is high in the mixed neighborhoods, where 22% of the residents belong to at least one such organization.

Participation in other voluntary organizations located in the neighborhood shows similar patterns. Twenty-nine percent of whites in strong-tie neighborhoods participate, compared to 25% of those living in weak-tie locations; 29% of the blacks in strong-tie neighborhoods belong, compared to 19% in weak-tie areas; and 23% of the residents in mixed neighborhoods are members of one or more of these organizations.

The results show that the white and black neighborhoods having relatively weak internal primary ties also have the lowest participation rates in voluntary organizations within the neighborhood. This is of concern for these neighborhoods because it shows a weaker basis from which to organize self-help activities; and because internal bonds are weaker, these neighborhoods may be in greater need of other types of institutional supports.

Happiness and Life Satisfaction

In white neighborhoods, residents in areas in which primary ties are more prevalent report slightly higher levels of life happiness than those living in locations having weaker internal bonds (22% versus 18% are very happy). The differences between these two groups in terms of life satisfaction are not large (approximately 85% of both groups report that they are satisfied or very satisfied).

In black neighborhoods, respondents in the strong-tie group report slightly higher levels of both happiness (16% versus 14%) and unhappiness (30% versus 24%) than those in the weak-tie group. Residents of black neighborhoods with a greater incidence of internal primary bonds are less satisfied with their life as a whole (78% report that they are satisfied or very satisfied compared to 86% in the weak-tie group).

Use of Neighborhood Facilities

In white neighborhoods with strong (weak) primary ties, 69% (48%) of residents do their main grocery shopping most or all of the time in or near the neighborhood, 51% (40%) shop for small items most or all of the time, and 64% (45%) attend religious services frequently. This compares to rates in strong-tie (weak-tie) black neighborhoods of 44% (50%), 28% (38%), and 37% (37%), respectively, for main grocery shopping, shopping for small items, and attending church services. In mixed neighborhoods the respective percentages are 67%, 44%, and 40%.

Shopping facilities are more readily available and used more often in the white neighborhoods in which primary bonds are more extensive and in the mixed subgroup than they are in the black neighborhoods. The white strong-tie neighborhoods make much greater use of neighborhood facilities than do the white neighborhoods in which primary bonds are not as prevalent. White and black weak-tie neighborhoods make comparable use of neighborhood shopping facilities, but neighborhood churches are used more frequently in the white subgroup.

Characteristics of Residents

Homeownership is higher in white neighborhoods having a greater incidence of primary bonds than it is in the white areas in which bonds are less strong (62% versus

52%); it is slightly higher in the weak-tie black neighborhoods than in the stronger ones (68% compared to 62%); and it is the lowest in the mixed neighborhoods (50%). Median household income follows a similar pattern. In the white neighborhoods, it is higher in the locations with strong ties ($11,170 versus $9,580) and in the black subgroups it is higher in the weak-tie locations ($11,110 versus $9,310). The average length of time lived in the neighborhood is higher in locations with a higher rather than lower incidence of primary bonds, 29 years compared to 22 in the white and 21 years versus 18 in the black subgroup. (Median household income and average tenure of the residents are $10,060 and 19 years, respectively, in the mixed neighborhood classification.)

The primary distinguishing characteristic between the two white subgroups is religion. Seventy-two percent of the population in the strong-tie neighborhoods is Catholic, compared to only 43% in the weak-tie neighborhoods. The dominant religion in the black and mixed groups is Protestant (approximately three-quarters of the population in the black neighborhoods). The importance of the Catholic population for the neighborhood was shown in the previous section. Churchgoing in or near the neighborhood is more prevalent in the white strong-tie subgroup than in any of the others.

Discussion

The strongest communal bonds exist within white, Catholic neighborhoods. Residents have the strongest primary ties there; they are more attached to their neighborhoods, and they rate them more positively than do residents in the other neighborhoods within the moderate-income group. Churchgoing occurs more frequently in white ethnic neighborhoods, participation in voluntary organizations is higher, neighboring occurs more often, homeownership is slightly higher, and residents have lived there a longer period of time than in other locations. In short, these neighborhoods have a number of attributes which attract their residents and evoke their commitments.

Although the white, Catholic neighborhoods show a stronger social fabric than the other white areas, there is not so large an apparent distinction between the strong-tie and weak-tie black neighborhoods. Primary bonds in the strong-tie black neighborhoods are more prevalent, attachment levels are higher, and participation in voluntary organizations is more extensive than in the weak-tie black neighborhoods, but neighborhood satisfaction is not higher and the institutional base of the neighborhoods in this subgroup is less strong. In a positive light, however, the homeownership rate in all black neighborhoods in this income group is high.

White, ethnically mixed neighborhoods in this income group do not have a common religious bond to bind the residents together, and the implications of this fact are seen in terms of a weaker social fabric and less of a sense of community. The same conclusion applies to the black neighborhoods, but the explanation is not so straightforward. Most of the black respondents reported an affiliation with a Protestant religion, but this covers a wide variety of denominations; therefore, there is not so strong a unifying religious base in these neighborhoods as there is in the white Catholic neighborhoods. Also, black neighborhoods, as compared to the white, are less likely to have a place of worship in or near the neighborhood.

The relationship between the strength of the neighborhood's primary ties and the happiness and life satisfaction of the residents is a little ambiguous. In white neighborhoods, life satisfaction levels do not vary among the two groups of neighborhoods, but happiness is higher in the strong-tie locations, whereas in black neighborhoods life satisfaction is lower in the areas in which internal ties are more prevalent.

LOWER-INCOME NEIGHBORHOODS

Eleven neighborhoods fall into the lowest-income category. These are predominantly renter neighborhoods (homeownership for the group is 39%), with a low level of resident satisfaction (45% of the respondents in this group rate their neighborhood good or excellent, compared to a sample average of 72%). The mean length of time lived in these neighborhoods is one year more than the city-wide average, but it is lower than the city mean in six of the eleven neighborhoods. Neighboring activities occur less often than they do for the city as a whole in eight neighborhoods and the level for this subgroup overall shows a decline from the moderate-income group. Attachment to the neighborhood for this group is only slightly less than it is for the three other groups. (Table 42 contains statistics for each neighborhood in the lower-income group.)

Primary ties in these neighborhoods show a mixed pattern compared to the other income groups. In all neighborhoods, except for the North Shore, the percentage of residents with their best social friend living in the neighborhood equals or exceeds the city average. For the group as a whole, 60% of the respondents have their best social friend living in the neighborhood, the highest percentage of any of the income groups. The percentage of respondents with relatives living in the neighborhood declined from that of the middle- and moderate-income groups, but it is still higher than that of the upper-income group (four neighborhoods in the lower-income group have higher percentages than the city average). The provider of emotional supports is less likely to live in the neighborhood in the lower-income group than in the moderate category, but more likely than in the upper-income group (four lower-income neighborhoods have percentages above the city average).

For a further analysis of these neighborhoods, they were classified into subgroups based upon the strength of

Table 42. Low-Income Neighborhoods: Selected Statistics[a]

Neighborhood	Percentage living in neighborhood			Neighboring[b]	Use of neighborhood facilities[c]	Percentage attached to neighborhood[d]	Percentage satisfied with neighborhood[e]	Average number of years in neighborhood	Percentage of homeownership	Percentage of blacks/Catholics/Jews
	Relatives	Best social friend	Provider of emotional support							
North Shore	42%	42%	20%	66	118	57%	42%	25	21%	64% (C)
North View Heights	45	60	33	79	100	55	44	18	22	60 (B)
Arlington Heights	36	70	16	74	114	63	47	18	26	66 (B)
Strip District	50	57	40	81	101	71	46	35	57	30 (B)
Homewood West	40	63	45	73	105	66	43	20	58	86 (B)
Oakland-Lower	34	60	20	79	134	48	47	16	30	49 (C)
Hill District-Lower	39	61	29	69	119	67	50	26	54	92 (B)
Hill District-Middle	52	64	38	67	111	63	37	27	51	98 (B)
Terrace Village	34	55	27	66	109	59	49	17	21	93 (B)
Bedford Dwellings	52	69	30	69	102	64	47	26	24	97 (B)
Bluff	37	55	28	75	108	46	41	20	42	35 (B)
Total group	41	60	30	71	113	60	45	22	39	71 (B)
Total city	44	55	32	79	119	63	72	21	63	22 (B)

[a]This group includes all neighborhoods with mean household income more than one standard deviation below the city mean.
[b]The figure shown is the value of the neighboring index for each neighborhood. See footnote b of Table 36 for explanation.
[c]The figure shown is the value of the neighborhood facilities use index for each neighborhood. See footnote of Table 36 for explanation.
[d]Percentage of respondents strongly or very strongly attached to the neighborhood.
[e]Percentage of respondents rating the neighborhood a good or excellent place to live.

their primary ties using the classification procedure described in the previous section. An additional stratification based upon the racial composition of the neighborhood was not undertaken because all but three of the neighborhoods were predominantly black. Six neighborhoods fall into the weak primary tie category and five into the strong-tie subgroup.

The strong-tie subgroups have a slightly higher median income ($7,270 compared to $6,160), a higher percentage of black population (86% versus 61%), and a higher homeownership rate (43% versus 36%). Residents of these neighborhoods have lived there longer (25 versus 21 years) and are older (55 versus 51 years of age) than those in the weak-tie areas. Further, membership in the organizations that address neighborhood problems is more prevalent in strong-tie neighborhoods (21% compared to 14% in the weaker locations), and participation in other types of neighborhood voluntary organizations also occurs at slightly higher rates in those locations having stronger primary bonds (27% versus 22%). Finally, residents of these areas report slightly stronger neighborhood attachments (63%, compared to 58%, are strongly attached). These statistics show, not surprisingly, that neighborhoods with the least internal social strength are those having the lowest income, least homeownership, and lowest average resident tenure.

The six neighborhoods in the weak primary-tie group are unusual to a certain extent. Two are predominantly public housing communities (Arlington Heights and Terrace Village); two are areas in which a large amount of property acquisition and demolition has occurred as a result of city urban renewal programs (North Shore and Lower Hill); one (Lower Oakland) is adjacent to the University of Pittsburgh and has experienced significant inroads into its residential base as a result of expansion by the University; and the last one (Bluff) is on the periphery of downtown, adjacent to Duquesne University and has been subject to significant urban renewal activity. In short,

the internal dynamics and social fabric of each neighborhood have been adversely influenced by the actions of an
external force.

It is not possible to conclude from this discussion that
the intervention of an outside force is always disruptive to
the social fabric; North View Heights is predominantly a
public housing neighborhood, but values of its three primary-tie variables exceed city averages.

The analysis in this section highlights the importance
of incorporating exogenous variables into the analysis of
individual neighborhoods. The actions, or threat of action,
by public, private, or nonprofit institutions may change the
internal dynamics of a neighborhood, thereby weakening
the social fabric.

CONCLUSION

A few general observations flow from the discussion in
this chapter. As the income level of the neighborhood falls,
the satisfaction of residents within the neighborhood
declines, neighboring occurs less frequently, participation
rates decline slightly, but primary bonds within the neighborhood generally increase, although not for all neighborhoods in the lowest-income category. Levels of happiness
and life satisfaction are directly related to the income level
of the neighborhood, falling as income decreases. Neighborhood attachment was not found to differ significantly
among the four income categories, but it did vary among
neighborhoods within each of the four groups with higher
attachment levels being related to stronger primary ties
within the neighborhood.

Associated with declining income levels were decreas-
ing homeownership rates (except for the middle-income
group, which showed an increase), and longer resident tenure. These variables were not uniform across all neighborhoods within each of the four subgroups, and differences
among neighborhoods along these dimensions were associated with variations in the strength of primary ties in the

neighborhood. In the middle-income group, higher levels of neighboring and a greater prevalence of primary ties were found in those neighborhoods where resident tenure and homeownership were higher than in other neighborhoods. Within the moderate-income group, white neighborhoods in the strong-tie subgroup had higher homeownership rates and longer resident tenure than those in the weak-tie group. For black neighborhoods, a slightly lower homeownership rate was found in the strong-tie neighborhoods, but residents had lived in these areas longer than they had in the weak-tie locations. In the lowest-income neighborhoods, homeownership and tenure were higher in the neighborhoods in which primary bonds were more prevalent. These two neighborhood characteristics, therefore, help to build a stronger social fabric.

The ethnic characteristics of the neighborhood, as captured by the percentage of the population which is Catholic, also have important implications for the nature of the social relationships that occur within the neighborhood. This is particularly evident for neighborhoods in the moderate-income group. Neighborhoods exhibiting strong primary ties within this classification had a predominantly Catholic population and significant church attendance. Neighborhoods in the middle-income group which displayed strong primary ties also had a greater Catholic population than those that had weak ties, but the differences in the percentage of Catholics among the neighborhoods in this group were not so pronounced as they were for the neighborhoods in the moderate-income category. The religious nature of the neighborhood was not an important variable in describing neighborhood differences in the high-income group, or the low-income group, in which most of the neighborhoods were predominantly black.

The racial character of the neighborhood is also associated with the prevalence of primary ties. In the moderate-income group, for instance, primary ties are less strong in the neighborhoods having a predominantly black population.

From the standpoint of maintaining a healthy, strong

neighborhood, as the income level of the residents falls, the social and institutional base of the neighborhood becomes more important. The analysis of neighborhoods within the moderate-income group clearly demonstrates the importance of the ethnic character of the neighborhood. White neighborhoods which are ethnically strong have a more cohesive social fabric and a stronger institutional base than the rest.

Neighborhoods in the lowest income category are predominantly black, their institutional base is not so strong as neighborhoods in the other income categories, and their social fabric is weaker than it is in many other locations. Although a greater percentage of residents in this income group have their best social friend living in the neighborhood than is the case for other income groups, this is most likely a result of the lack of income restricting the individual's locus of activity and is not necessarily a sign of neighborhood strength. Residents of these lower-income areas are slightly less likely than those in moderate- and middle-income areas to have relatives or their provider of emotional supports living there. Also, many of the weaker neighborhoods in this income group have had their social fabric disrupted by an external event (public housing, urban renewal).

The discussion in this chapter underscores the importance of analyzing neighborhoods on an individual basis in order to discern their contextual differences. Each neighborhood within each income category is unique in many respects. Differences in income, homeownership, tenure, race, and ethnicity lead to variations in the strength of the social fabric which is, in the final analysis, the critical element for the health of the residents and the vitality of the neighborhood. As the income level of the neighborhood declines and the institutional base is eroded away or never existed in the first place, the social cohesion of the neighborhood is all that the residents have to fall back on in attempting to maintain a vital community. From this perspective, several of the neighborhoods in the moderate-income group and many of those in the lower-income group are in some difficulty. They lack income, institutions, and a strong social fabric; therefore it is difficult to see how they will be able to stem decline unless outside assistance is made available and institutional building occurs within their boundaries.

This chapter examined a number of different aspects of the neighborhood from the perspective of income, and the conclusion that there are structural effects operating among the groups is similar to that of Chapter 8. This chapter, however, took the analysis one step further and compared neighborhoods within each of the four income groups, and found that contextual effects differ within each group as well.

Neighborhood analysis must therefore incorporate contextual effects in order to assess strengths and weaknesses, and this can only be done at the microlevel by looking at individual neighborhoods. Certainly income and race make a difference, but so does ethnicity, the lack of homeownership, average length of time lived in the neighborhood, availability and use of institutions, and so on. The characteristics of the residents and the institutional base have an effect on, or at least are associated with, differences among neighborhoods in terms of the strength of their social fabric, and all of these variables must be considered in any discussion of community.

The findings in this chapter show that community can be constructed by a number of the variables that form the contextual environment of the neighborhood. The institutional base—particularly the presence of a strong organization, such as the Catholic church—provides a mechanism which draws people inward and helps to create and maintain the neighborhood's social fabric. This illustrates the benefits which accrue to the neighborhood if it offers its residents a strong incentive to participate. If residents have a reason for involving themselves in the neighborhood, they are likely to help build the interpersonal dimensions which are essential to the neighborhood's future.

Unless people are constrained to place because of lack of income or physical immobility, they will have significant choices of where to participate and where to maintain their personal relationships. Therefore, in light of the number of potential communities of action for many people, the neighborhood must be competitive in one respect or another if it is to attract its residents inward and thereby elicit a commitment from them.

The contextual effects of the neighborhood can be interpreted in terms of the choice-constraint model. Certain contextual variables—such as race, ethnicity, income, institutions—influence the choices that people have and constrain their behavior. Therefore, the neighborhood context should be thought of in terms of its influence on the choices that people have and its contribution to the related attractiveness of the neighborhood as a place in which to socialize and participate.

CHAPTER 10

The Neighborhood and Beyond

DISCUSSION

The research shows that neighborhoods are indeed communities of limited liability. People are attached to their own neighborhood and they also have commitments in the wider community. However, different groups of people are attached to their neighborhoods in different ways and for diverse reasons.

In order to explore the determinants of neighborhood involvement and the strength of communal ties, a choice-constraint model of human behavior was used. The model is based on the recognition that people's behavior is constrained by factors such as their socioeconomic status and that these constraints directly affect the choices upon which people have to act.

The model provided a useful framework in which to study community questions. Age, income, race, ethnicity, and household composition were shown to be important explanatory variables for ways in which people use the neighborhood and their attitudes toward it.

Within the framework provided by this model, the location of people's intimate ties was examined. This analysis showed that people living in all neighborhoods, even the lower-income areas, have significant external ties, and therefore the neighborhood is just one of the places in which an individual household's locus of activity occurs. However, for those who are more restricted to place (poor, elderly, households with children), the neighborhood assumes greater importance in their lives than it does for other households.

In general, dependence upon the neighborhood lessens as people's social, physical, and economic mobility increases. As their choices expand, the neighborhood has to compete with a variety of alternative locations for the commitment and involvement of the residents. It is therefore not surprising that the communal aspects of the neighborhood are related to the characteristics of the residents and their opportunity to participate in the wider community.

These findings show that some people choose to become involved in the neighborhood because the neighborhood offers a superior option for social interaction, shopping, worship, and the like. Others—the elderly, the poor, and blacks—are more place-bound and may use the neighborhood simply because it is their only alternative.

People, having options of where to spend their time and energy, will only be drawn into a neighborhood if it meets their needs. Therefore, in one sense, neighborhoods may be thought of as being in competition with one another. If a neighborhood offers a better product than alternative locations, it will draw its residents inward; if it does not, they will go outside of the neighborhood to meet their needs and satisfy their wants.

Neighborhood life has a variety of dimensions, and where these features of the neighborhood—personal, physical, and institutional—offer strong inducements for involvement, communal feelings will be high. When neighborhoods provide disincentives for involvement by their residents, the sense of community will be low. Therefore, the neighborhood, and not just the residents, plays an important role in constructing community. The community can be strong in neighborhoods in which residents have extensive external ties if it encourages involvement, and it can be weak in neighborhoods in which the residents have few external ties if it discourages involvement.

The key to the construction of community within neighborhoods is the willingness of residents to become involved, and this depends in part upon the incentives—the costs and benefits—provided by the neighborhood for participation. Neighborhoods having a strong institutional base—particularly the presence of a church or synagogue—and those offering a high quality of life can create an environment in which community flourishes. Neighborhoods that do not offer positive inducements for involvement will have a weak communal base.

Neighborhoods, in conjunction with the residents, can therefore be thought of as creating community. The services provided by the neighborhood, the characteristics of the residents, and the social and emotional ties within the neighborhood are factors which influence the feelings that people have about their place of residence. It is a combination of all of these factors that determines the strength of the communal bonds within the neighborhood.

The research findings also show that there are different types of affective sentiments. The attachment and loyalty that people have to the neighborhood differ from their satisfaction with the neighborhood as a place to live. Feelings of attachment and loyalty that people have to the neighborhood differ from their satisfaction with the neighborhood as a place to live. Feelings of attachment and loyalty are influenced to a much greater extent by the social fabric of the neighborhood, whereas neighborhood satisfaction depends more on the physical aspects of the neighborhood and the services it provides. This difference is readily explicable in terms of the choices and constraints people face. Individuals with the greatest mobility are not so restricted to place as those who have fewer options of where to live and those who cannot as readily maintain contacts outside their neighborhood. It stands to reason that satisfaction with the neighborhood will be highest for those who have the greatest range of economic choice—they would move if they were not as satisfied; and because these people have the greatest ability to maintain personal contacts over a wide geographic area, it is not surprising that their attachment to the neighborhood is less intense.

The research findings underscore the following important points about the community question in an urban setting:

- There are a number of different types of communal bonds ranging from simple neighboring to intimate ties which provide emotional support in times of need.
- People use the neighborhood for a variety of things, including interpersonal contacts, participation in voluntary organizations, shopping, and churchgoing, and all of these contribute to their sense of community.
- These uses vary by the socioeconomic characteristics of the residents because factors such as age, income, and ethnicity influence peoples' choices.
- Community is created by an interaction of the residents and the neighborhood.
- The neighborhood plays an important role in this process; it offers a quality of life and opportunities for social interaction which, if valued by the residents, exert a pull inward which helps to create commitment and participation; if not valued, the residents may choose to socialize and participate outside of the neighborhood, and their relevant community of action will be the wider community; for those with few alternatives, the neighborhood provides perhaps the only opportunity for social and institutional interaction.
- The Catholic neighborhoods, particularly those within the moderate-income group, best illustrate the positive effects of a strong incentive for neighborhood participation. The presence of an active church pulls the residents inward and evokes strong neighborhood commitments. This is seen in strong

primary ties within the neighborhood, frequent neighboring, high rates of participation in voluntary organizations, and infrequent resident turnover; communal bonds are high in these locations.

- Attachment to the neighborhood—evidence of the strength of community—is influenced by a number of factors but is related to the social interaction and the presence of primary ties within the neighborhood; satisfaction with the neighborhood as a place to live is more closely related to the physical attributes of the neighborhood; each of these sentiments is influenced by the choices and constraints which the residents face.

- Attachment to the neighborhood generally increases as people's income falls and their opportunity to maintain contacts outside the neighborhood lessens; but this is not true for the lower-income neighborhoods where a number of factors, including public intervention, have undermined the fabric of social life within the neighborhood.

- The presence of a social support system is directly related to an individual's happiness and life satisfaction. Respondents having more close friends, neighboring more often, and/or having a spouse are happier and more satisfied with life. The neighborhood plays a role in these feelings as well. Those who use the neighborhood for shopping, worship, recreation, and participation in voluntary organizations are happier and more satisfied with life than those who do not.

- People's satisfaction with the neighborhood and their overall happiness with their life are directly related to income; as income rises, neighborhood satisfaction and life happiness do also; this indicates that as peoples' options rise they are able to make choices which better meet their needs.

- As the income level of the neighborhood falls, its internal structure—people and institutions—

becomes more important to the residents; black neighborhoods, particularly in the lowest income group, are most at risk; their institutional structure is not so strong as it is in other locations, and the personal support systems within these neighborhoods are weaker.

● For lower-income neighborhoods, those with the strongest institutional base are more likely to show other strengths as well, particularly a more vibrant real estate market.

The research findings are important because they provide insights into the complicated nature of community in an urban setting. They also show how productive avenues of research into this question can be fashioned in terms of a choice-constraint framework as well as the uses of social network analysis to pinpoint the actual location of people's different communities of action.

POLICY IMPLICATIONS

Neighborhoods are shown to be unique along a number of important dimensions, including their institutional base, personal support networks, housing stock, characteristics of the residents, specific problems, and the attachment felt by the population. Because of these differences, the strengths and weaknesses will vary; therefore, policies must be tailored to the individual circumstances of specific neighborhoods. Having made this point, we can present a few general observations for public policymakers who are concerned with strengthening neighborhoods to make them less susceptible to unwanted change and for those concerned with developing approaches to mental health prevention by shoring up the ability of people to cope with stress.

The individuals within urban areas who are the most vulnerable to the stresses of everyday living are those who not only have inadequate economic resources but who also lack strong institutional and social supports. These conditions are disproportionately concentrated among lower-income people, the elderly, and blacks and the neighborhoods in which they live. Lack of income limits people's choices of where to live and their mobility once they are in place; therefore, lower-income individuals depend more on their place of residence to meet their needs than do those having greater economic resources. If the neighborhoods in which lower-income people reside are deficient in terms of their institutional structure, then these residents have fewer alternatives to fall back on in times of crisis, and the neighborhood has fewer internal strengths to resist forces of decay.

Being constrained to place, for whatever the reason, increases people's reliance upon the neighborhood, its services, and the fabric of its social life. A supportive environment may be provided by neighbors, friends, or family living in the area and the nearby institutions. In the absence of personal or institutional supports, the individual must cope as best he or she can, using whatever personal resources are available. Obviously, if personal resources are deficient, other supports become more important for the individual.

The research findings show that the strength of the primary bonds within neighborhoods increases as income falls, and this is a positive occurrence; however, there are a few neighborhoods where this is not the case. In these areas, concentrated in the lowest-income neighborhoods with a few in the moderate-income category, institutions are lacking in a relative sense, homeownership is low, neighboring is infrequent, primary ties are relatively weak, and the nuclear family is not particularly evident. As a result, these neighborhoods lack the inherent strength and social cohesion necessary to combat the stresses imposed on either the resident or the neighborhood.

If public policy is to be directed successfully toward these communities, it must take into account the strengths and the deficiencies in the personal and institutional networks within these neighborhoods. Whether the issue is mental health prevention or neighborhood stabilization, the intervention strategy must be both place- and people-oriented. The treatment of the individual requires rectifying the negative aspects of place, which include a lack of institutions and a deficient physical environment. Alternatively, the treatment of place requires a recognition that a healthy community is built upon a strong institutional and social structure and that, if these aspects of place are weak or deficient, they must be strengthened as well.

This approach to mental health prevention policy and to neighborhood and community renewal requires the flexibility to adapt to the unique aspects of both an individual's and a neighborhood's support structure. It also necessitates comprehensiveness in the sense of treating not only the symptoms (the depressed individual or the decaying housing stock), but also the environment of the resident (strengthening the support network) and the neighborhood (social and institutional structure).

A component of such a strategy is the development of viable voluntary institutions in the neighborhood. This is an attempt to support or help to build an institution which can emulate the positive effects ascribed to the Catholic Church in many of the middle- and moderate-income neighborhoods in this study. Such an organization provides a focal point for community interaction and will help develop a stronger social fabric, thereby strengthening the communal bonds within the neighborhood. Examples of approaches to strengthening the social fabric and institutional structure include the following:

● Assistance for institutions which provide a focal point for bringing people together, such as community organizations, recreation centers, and senior citizen centers.
● Funding for specific programs which bring people together, such as recreational or cultural activities and ethnic fairs.

- Funding community organizers to help build a neighborhood organization or to help create programs for serving people who are in need. For example, programs which bring widows together for discussions of common problems or activities involving sewing and the like could be undertaken.
- Helping to develop or sustain neighborhood newspapers.
- Ensuring that a mixture of housing is maintained in the neighborhood so that younger households with children and their aging parents can live in the same neighborhood.
- Providing assistance to neighborhood commercial areas in order to keep them from decaying.
- Providing technical assistance to all types of voluntary organizations in a neighborhood, if necessary, to keep them healthy.
- Developing new institutions, where needed, to meet specific problems of a given population group, such as mental health outreach centers.
- Encouraging the development and maintenance of networks that bring together people and groups that have specialized knowledge and skills with those individuals and organizations in need of assistance.

The objectives of these examples are to support the voluntary and self-help activities of residents within the neighborhood; to strengthen the social fabric of the neighborhood by raising the level of interaction among residents through bringing people together more often and thus facilitating increased communication; and to augment the institutional structure of the neighborhood by helping existing institutions to operate more effectively, to aid them in reaching out into the neighborhood, or by bringing in new institutions to serve unmet needs.

Another policy direction is to focus on enhancing the options that people have for satisfying their needs. The research demonstrates that peoples' satisfaction with their neighborhood and their feelings about their life are directly related to income. Thus, people who have sufficient resources are more likely to be able to select that alternative which best satisfies their personal circumstances. Income assistance programs that augment the choices of the recipient should be pursued. An example of such an approach is the substitution of a housing voucher for the traditional housing subsidy programs which attach the subsidy to a specific unit in a specific location. The voucher would cover part of the rent for the recipient of any rental unit selected regardless of location. This would increase the housing choices of recipients and therefore give them the opportunity to select from among a larger number of neighborhoods. This expands their options and gives them the opportunity to live in a neighborhood which offers them not only the best housing they can afford but also the types of personal and institutional supports they desire.

The key to the success of these strategies is to develop strong links between individuals and between individuals and institutions. By developing stronger networks, the coping ability of both the individual and the neighborhood will be augmented and the communal base of the neighborhood will be strengthened.

It is recognized that the building of individual and institutional networks will be difficult to accomplish. However, the acknowledgment that this is needed is an important first step, and it may at least keep public policymakers from destroying or undermining existing networks.

This book is an extension of existing research into neighborhoods and their people. Its function has been to demonstrate the importance of place and the variety of ties and support systems existing in the urban area. Clearly, further research, specifically action-oriented research, is needed to determine which types of strategies work best, and under what conditions, to sustain strengths or to enhance the existing social and institutional structure of urban neighborhoods and the support systems of their residents.

The findings of this study suggest that appropriate policies should involve those that are both people- and place-oriented. The people-focused efforts should be designed to increase the options of people to participate in personal and institutional networks that best satisfy their needs. The strategies directed toward place will also be required because many of those confined to place have few other options of where to live.

Much remains to be learned about the conditions under which institutions of various types can play an important role in neighborhood life. The role of government should be to help fund the research, disseminate information on effective models, remove barriers to the formation and operation of these organizations, provide appropriate incentives to stimulate their development, and provide resources as needed.

APPENDIX C

Survey Questionnaire

NEIGHBORHOOD SUPPORT STUDY

Name of Neighborhood: _____

Census Tract: _____

Address: _____

Telephone Number: _____

Date of Interview: _____

Time Interview Begins: _____

Time Interview Ends: _____

Length of Interview: _____

Interviewer: _____

Section I: Sense of Community

FIRST, I WANT TO ASK YOU ABOUT THIS NEIGHBORHOOD . . .

1. When people ask you the name of the neighborhood, what name do
you usually give?

_____ (RECORD NAME)

Gave clear name 2
Gave vague name 1
Doesn't know (DK) .. 8
No Answer (NA) 9

1. _____

2. How long have you lived in this neighborhood? _____ (RECORD IN YRS) 2. _____

3. How long have you lived in this home (apartment)?

_____ (RECORD IN YRS) 3. _____

4. Thinking of _____: (USE NEIGHBORHOOD NAME)

		Yes	**No**	**DK**	**NA**	
a.	Does it claim a greater loyalty from you than the rest of the city?	1	0	8	9	4a. _____
b.	Does it have particular activities solely for residents?	1	0	8	9	4b. _____
c.	Does it have definite boundaries?	1	0	8	9	4c. _____

5. Why did you move to this neighborhood? (DO NOT READ RESPONSES;
    CIRCLE THE MOST IMPORTANT REASON)

    Other 13
    Born, raised here 12
    Spouse lived here 11
    Family lived here 10
    Friends lived here 09
    Good location, convenient 08
    Better neighborhood, nice neighborhood 07
    Reasonable housing prices (rents) 06
    Better home (apartment) 05
    Good schools 04
    Good public services (recreation) 03
    Good place to raise kids 02
    Safe neighborhood 01
    DK 98
    NA 99   5. _____

6. Do you have relatives living in this neighborhood?

                        Yes 1
                        No 0
                        DK 8
                        NA 9   6. _____

7. When you think of your attachment to this neighborhood, are you
    very strongly attached, strongly attached, undecided, not strongly
    attached, or not at all attached?

                        Very strongly 5
                        Strongly 4
                        Undecided 3
                        Not strongly 2
                        Not at all 1
                        DK 8
                        NA 9   7. _____

Section II: Local Facility Use

NOW I WOULD LIKE TO ASK YOU A FEW QUESTIONS ABOUT ACTIVITIES YOU
MAY DO IN OR NEAR YOUR NEIGHBORHOOD, AND BY NEAR I MEAN WITHIN A
FIVE-MINUTE DRIVE.

8. Is there a grocery store in or near your neighborhood?

                        Yes 1
                        No 0
                        DK .... 8 ┐──► Skip to
                        NA .... 9 ┘   Q10   8. _____

9. (If YES) How often do you do your main grocery shopping there?
    (READ RESPONSES)
                        All 4
                        Most 3
                        Some 2
                        None 1
                        Inappropriate 7
                        DK 8
                        NA 9   9. _____

10. Are there other stores at which you can shop for small items in or near your neighborhood?

Yes 1
No 0
DK .... 8 → Skip to
NA 9   Q12

10. _____

11. How often do you use these stores for your shopping, dry cleaning and so on?

All 4
Most 3
Some 2
None 1
Inappropriate 7
DK 8
NA 9

11. _____

12. Is there a church or synagogue which you could attend in or near your neighborhood?

Yes 1
No 0
DK .... 8 → Skip to
NA 9   Q14

12. _____

13. (If YES) How often do you attend services there? All of the time, most of the time, some of the time or not at all?

All 4
Most 3
Some 2
None 1
Inappropriate 7
DK 8
NA 9

13. _____

14. Are health or medical services available in or near your neighborhood?

Yes 1
No 0
DK .... 8 → Skip to
NA 9   Q16

14. _____

15. When you need these services, how often will you use the ones available in or near your neighborhood?

All 4
Most 3
Some 2
None 1
Inappropriate 7
DK 8
NA 9

15. _____

16. Are recreational activities, such as a recreation center, movies, swimming, or bowling, available in or near your neighborhood?

Yes 1
No 0
DK .... 8 → Skip to
NA 9   Q18

16. _____

17. How often do you use these facilities?

All 4
Most 3
Some 2
None 1
Inappropriate 7
DK 8
NA 9

17. _____

Section III: Neighborhood Conditions

THINKING ABOUT CONDITIONS IN THE TWO OR THREE BLOCKS RIGHT
AROUND YOUR HOME ....

18. If you had to pick one problem that you consider the most serious
    in your neighborhood, what problem would that be?

    _____   18. _____

19. What is the one thing about this neighborhood that you like best?

    _____   19. _____

20. I will mention some neighborhood conditions and would like you
    to tell me if they are a major problem, a minor problem or not
    a problem in your neighborhood. (READ EACH CONDITION)

		Major Problem	Minor Problem	Not a Problem	DK	NA	
a.	Vacant buildings	3	2	1	8	9	20a._____
b.	Deteriorated buildings ..	3	2	1	8	9	20b._____
c.	Cost of housing	3	2	1	8	9	20c._____
d.	Vandalism	3	2	1	8	9	20d._____
e.	Burglaries	3	2	1	8	9	20e._____
f.	Muggings	3	2	1	8	9	20f._____
g.	Rats	3	2	1	8	9	20g._____
h.	Undesirable people	3	2	1	8	9	20h._____
i.	Litter and garbage	3	2	1	8	9	20i._____
j.	Stray dogs	3	2	1	8	9	20j._____
k.	Street maintenance	3	2	1	8	9	20k._____

21. Looking back over the past year or two, would you say that
    conditions in this neighborhood have:

    > Improved 3
    > Stayed the same 2
    > Declined 1
    > DK 8
    > NA 9   21. _____

22. In general, how would you rate this neighborhood as a place
    to live? Is it:

    > Excellent 4
    > Good 3
    > Fair 2
    > Poor 1
    > DK 8
    > NA 9   22. _____

23. Taking all things together, how would you say things are these
    days--would you say you are very happy, pretty happy or not too
    happy?

    > Very happy 3
    > Pretty happy 2
    > Not too happy 1
    > DK 8
    > NA 9   23. _____

Section IV: Willingness to Remain in the Neighborhood

24. As things look to you now, do you plan to move in the next two years?

    > Yes 1
    > No .... 0 ⎤
    > DK .... 8 ⎬ ➤ Skip to
    > NA .... 9 ⎦   Q27   24. _____

25. (If YES) Why do you plan to move?

_____

_____

_____   25. _____

26. Where do you plan to move?   (DO NOT READ RESPONSES)

On this street to another home 6
Elsewhere in this neighborhood 5
To another neighborhood in
    the city 4
Out of the city into a suburb
    in the county 3
Out of Allegheny County but
    in Pennsylvania 2
Out of Pennsylvania entirely 1
Inappropriate 7
DK 8
NA 9   26. _____

Section V: Neighboring Patterns

NOW I WOULD LIKE TO ASK YOU A FEW QUESTIONS ABOUT THE PEOPLE
LIVING IN THIS NEIGHBORHOOD . . .

27. How often do you borrow or exchange things with your neighbors?
     Often, sometimes, rarely or never?

Often 4
Sometimes 3
Rarely 2
Never 1
DK 8
NA 9   27. _____

28. How often do you visit with your neighbors? Often, sometimes,
     rarely or never?

Often 4
Sometimes 3
Rarely 2
Never 1
DK 8
NA 9   28. _____

29. Within the past year, how often have people in this neighborhood
     helped you or you helped them with small tasks, such as repair
     work or grocery shopping? Often, sometimes, rarely or never?

Often 4
Sometimes 3
Rarely 2
Never 1
DK 8
NA 9   29. _____

30. If an emergency arose in your home such as an accident requiring
     assistance of adults, could you call on your neighbors for help?

Yes 1
No 0
DK .... 8 ──► Skip to
NA 9   Q32   30. _____

31. (If YES) About how many of your neighbors would help you?

_____ (RECORD NUMBER)   31. _____

32. Do you feel that you have a lot in common with your neighbors,
    a little, not much or nothing in common?

                        A lot 4
                        A little 3
                        Not much 2
                        Nothing 1
                        DK 8
                        NA 9   32. _____

Section VI: Social Supports: Socialization

NOW I WOULD LIKE TO ASK YOU A FEW QUESTIONS ABOUT YOUR FRIENDS . . .

33a. About how many people do you consider really good friends?

                        _____ (RECORD NUMBER)   33a._____

33b. About how many of these people live in your neighborhood?

                        _____ (RECORD NUMBER)   33b._____

34. Among your friends, which person do you socialize or visit with
    most often? Please give me just the first name or initial of
    this person. (IF ASKED, TELL THE RESPONDENT THAT YOU NEED THIS
    INFORMATION SO THAT YOU CAN ASK SOME FOLLOW-UP QUESTIONS ABOUT
    THAT PERSON; IF RESPONDENT REPLIES, "THE SMITHS," ASK HIM/HER
    TO IDENTIFY WHICH OF THE SMITHS IS MORE IMPORTANT.)

                        _____ (NAME OR INITIAL)

    NOW I WOULD LIKE TO ASK YOU A FEW QUESTIONS ABOUT _____. (IF
    NO NAMES ARE GIVEN, SKIP TO Q47.)

35. (If not clear) Is _____ male or female?

                        Male 1
                        Female 2
                        Inappropriate 7   35. _____

36. Is _____ a relative, co-worker, member of your church or
    other organization? (CIRCLE JUST ONE RESPONSE)

                        Relative 5
                        Co-worker 4
                        Member of church ... 3
                        Member other org ... 2
                        Other 1
                        Inappropriate 7
                        DK 8
                        NA 9   36. _____

37. About how many years have you known _____? _____ (RECORD YRS) 37. _____

38. How often do you usually get together with _____? (DO NOT READ RESPONSES)

                        About everyday 6
                        Once a week or more 5
                        Once a month or more 4
                        Several times a year 3
                        About once a year 2
                        Less than once a year ... 1
                        Inappropriate 7
                        DK 8
                        NA 9   38. _____

39. About how old is _____?   _____ (RECORD YEARS)   39. _____

40. Does _____ do the same kind of work (consider being a housewife
    work) as you do/did?
                                    Yes 1
                                    No 0
                                    Inappropriate 7
                                    DK 8
                                    NA 9   40. _____

41. Is _____ presently:
                                    Married 5
                                    Widowed 4
                                    Divorced 3
                                    Separated 2
                                    Never married 1
                                    Inappropriate 7
                                    DK 8
                                    NA 9   41. _____

42. Does _____ have children?

                                    Yes 1
                                    No 0
                                    Inappropriate 7
                                    DK 8
                                    NA 9   42. _____

43. What is _____'s ethnic (national) background?

                                    _____   43. _____

44. What is _____'s religion?
                                    _____   44. _____

45. Does _____ have more schooling than you do, about the same
    or less?
                                    More 3
                                    Same 2
                                    Less 1
                                    Inappropriate 7
                                    DK 8
                                    NA 9   45. _____

46. Where does _____ live? (DO NOT READ RESPONSES)

    In your neighborhood--say within a 10-
      minute walk of your home 5
    In the city but outside your neighborhood ... 4
    Outside of the city but in the Pittsburgh
      metropolitan area (within 25 miles of
      your home) 3
    Outside of the metropolitan area but
      in Pennsylvania 2
    Outside of Pennsylvania 1
    Inappropriate 7
    DK 8
    NA 9   46. _____

Section VII: Social Supports: Emotional Support

47. Normally when you are concerned about a personal matter, will you
    talk it over with someone? Often, sometimes, rarely or never?

                                    Often 4
                                    Sometimes 3
                                    Rarely 2
                                    Never 1
                                    DK .... 8 ⎤ Skip to
                                    NA .... 9 ⎦→ Q67   47. _____

48. When you do talk with someone about your personal concerns, whom
    do you talk with? Please give the first name or initials. (PROBE:
    Is there anyone else?) (RECORD "YES" OR "NO" ON EACH LINE.)

    a. Spouse .... Yes .... 1 ┐   48a._____
                            No .... 0 ├─► Skip to
    b. Person in Q34 ...... Yes .... 1 ┘   Q67   48b._____
                            No 0
    c. _____ Yes 1   48c._____
                            No 0
    d. _____ Yes 1   48d._____
                            No 0
    e. _____ Yes 1   48e._____
                            No 0
    f. _____ Yes 1   48f._____
                            No 0
    g. _____ Yes 1   48g._____
                            No 0

49. Of the people mentioned (OTHER THAN SPOUSE OR PERSON IN Q34), are
    any of them members of your household?

                        Yes 1
                        No .... 0 ──► Skip to Q53   49. _____

50. (If YES) How many are members of your household?

                        _____ (RECORD NUMBER)   50. _____

    NOW I WOULD LIKE TO ASK YOU SOME QUESTIONS ABOUT THAT PERSON.
    (IF MORE THAN ONE MEMBER OF THE HOUSEHOLD IS MENTIONED, ASK
    RESPONDENT FOR THE NAME OF THE PERSON WHO IS THE MOST IMPORTANT
    AND THEN ASK Q51 AND Q52 ABOUT THAT PERSON.)

                        1. _____

51. (If not clear) Is _____ male or female?

                        Male 1
                        Female 2
                        Inappropriate 7   51. _____

52. What is the relationship of _____ to you? (CIRCLE ONLY ONE)
    (DO NOT READ RESPONSES)
                        Grandfather 08
                        Grandmother 07
                        Father 06
                        Mother 05
                        Child 04
                        Relative 03
                        Friend 02
                        Other 01
                        Inappropriate 97
                        DK 98
                        NA 99   52. _____

53. Now I would like to ask you a few questions about _____ (NAMES
    MENTIONED IN Q48). Of those mentioned (OTHER THAN SPOUSE, MEMBER
    OF HOUSEHOLD OR PERSON IN Q34), who are the two that are closest
    to you? (LIST FIRST NAMES)

                        1. _____

                        2. _____   53. _____

    IF THE ONLY PEOPLE MENTIONED BY RESPONDENT ARE SPOUSE, PERSON IN
    Q34 AND/OR OTHER MEMBERS OF THE HOUSEHOLD, SKIP TO Q67.

(ASK EACH QUESTION [Q54-Q66] FOR THE TWO PEOPLE MENTIONED IN Q53)

54. (If not clear) Is _____ male or female?

	#1	#2
Male	1	1
Female	2	2
Inappropriate	7	7

(#1) 54a._____

(#2) 54b._____

55. What is your relationship to _____? Is he/she a relative, co-worker, neighbor or member of some organization? (CIRCLE ONLY ONE FOR EACH RESPONDENT)

	#1	#2	
Grandfather	17	17	
Grandmother	16	16	
Father	15	15	Skip to
Mother	14	14	Q64
Child	13	13	
Brother/Sister	12	12	
Relative	11	11	
Co-worker	10	10	
Neighbor	09	09	
Member of neighborhood org ...	08	08	
Member of church	07	07	
Member of other org	06	06	
Friend	05	05	Ask Q56-
Minister, priest, rabbi	04	04	Q66
Doctor	03	03	
Counselor	02	02	
Other	01	01	
Inappropriate	97	97	
DK	98	98	
NA	99	99	

(#1) 55a._____

(#2) 55b._____

(BE SURE TO CONTINUE TO CODE RESPONSES UNDER THE APPROPRIATE COLUMN HEADING; IF #1 FALLS WITHIN CATEGORIES 12-17 AND #2 DOES NOT, MAKE SURE THAT ALL RESPONSES FOR Q56-Q66 ARE CODED FOR #2; IF BOTH PEOPLE FALL WITHIN CATEGORIES 12-17, SKIP TO Q67.)

56. About how many years have you known _____?

#1 _____   #2 _____

(#1) 56a._____
(#2) 56b._____

57. About how old is _____?

#1 _____   #2 _____

(#1) 57a._____
(#2) 57b._____

58. Does _____ do the same kind of work (consider being a housewife work) as you do/did?

	#1	#2
Yes	1	1
No	0	0
Inappropriate	7	7
DK	8	8
NA	9	9

(#1) 58a._____

(#2) 58b._____

59. Is _____ presently:

	#1	#2
Married	5	5
Widowed	4	4
Divorced	3	3
Separated	2	2
Never married	1	1
Inappropriate	7	7
DK	8	8
NA	9	9

(#1) 59a._____

(#2) 59b._____

60. Does _____ have children?

	#1	#2
Yes	T	T
No	0	0
Inappropriate	7	7
DK	8	8
NA	9	9

(#1) 60a._____

(#2) 60b._____

61. What is _____'s ethnic (national) background?

    #1 _____   #2 _____

(#1) 61a._____
(#2) 61b._____

62. What is _____'s religion?

    #1 _____   #2 _____

(#1) 62a._____
(#2) 62b._____

63. Does _____ have more schooling than you do, about the same or less?

	#1	#2
More	3	3
Same	2	2
Less	1	1
Inappropriate	7	7
DK	8	8
NA	9	9

(#1) 63a._____

(#2) 63b._____

64. Is your contact with _____ generally:

	#1	#2
In person	4	4
By phone	3	3
Mixture of phone/in person	2	2
By letter	1	1
Inappropriate	7	7
DK	8	8
NA	9	9

(#1) 64a._____

(#2) 64b._____

65. How often do you usually get together with _____? (DO NOT READ RESPONSES)

	#1	#2
About everyday	6	6
Once a week or more	5	5
Once a month or more	4	4
Several times a year	3	3
About once a year	2	2
Less than once a year	1	1
Inappropriate	7	7
DK	8	8
NA	9	9

(#1) 65a._____

(#2) 65b._____

66. Where does _____ live? (DO NOT READ RESPONSES)

	#1	#2
In your neighborhood--say within a 10-minute walk of your home	5	5
In the city but outside your neighborhood	4	4
Outside of the city but in the Pittsburgh metropolitan area (within 25 miles of your home)	3	3
Oustide of the metropolitan area but in Pennsylvania	2	2
Outside of Pennsylvania	1	1
Inappropriate	7	7
DK	8	8
NA	9	9

(#1) 66a._____

(#2) 66b._____

TURNING TO ORGANIZATIONS IN YOUR NEIGHBORHOOD . . .

Section VIII: Neighborhood Supports

67. Is there any organization or group in this neighborhood that
     deals with neighborhood issues or neighborhood problems?

                    Yes 1
                    No 0
                    DK 8   ➤ Skip to
                    NA 9   Q77   67. _____

68. (If YES) What is the name of the organization or group? (IF
     MORE THAN ONE, LIST UP TO THREE.)

     1. _____   (#1) 68a._____

     2. _____   (#2) 68b._____

     3. _____. (#3) 68c._____

69. How many of these organizations do you belong to? (IF ONLY
     ONE MENTIONED, ASK: "DO YOU BELONG TO THIS ORGANIZATION?")

                    Three 3
                    Two 2
                    One (Yes) 1
                    None (No) 0
                    Inappropriate 7   ➤ Skip to
                    DK 8   Q72
                    NA 9   69. _____

70. How many hours a month do you spend in meetings or activities
     of this organization? (IF MORE THAN ONE ORGANIZATION MENTIONED
     IN Q69, ASK THIS QUESTION FOR THE MOST IMPORTANT ORGANIZATION.)

                    _____ (RECORD ACTUAL NUMBER)   70. _____

71. For how long have you been a member of this organization?

                    _____ (RECORD ACTUAL YEARS & MONTHS) 71. _____

                    SKIP TO Q75

72. How many of these organizations do members of your household
     belong to? (IF ONLY ONE MENTIONED, ASK: "DOES ANYONE IN YOUR
     HOUSEHOLD BELONG TO THIS ORGANIZATION?")

                    Three 3
                    Two 2
                    One (Yes) 1
                    None (No) 0
                    Inappropriate 7
                    DK 8
                    NA 9   72. _____

73. How many hours a month does the most active member of your
     household spend in meetings or activities of this organization?
     (IF MORE THAN ONE ORGANIZATION MENTIONED IN Q72, ASK THIS QUES-
     TION FOR THE MOST IMPORTANT ORGANIZATION.)

                    _____ (RECORD ACTUAL NUMBER)   73. _____

74. For how long has this person been a member of this organization?

                    _____ (RECORD ACTUAL YEARS   74. _____
                                 AND MONTHS)

75. How satisfied are you with this organization in making the
    neighborhood a better place to live?   (DO NOT READ RESPONSES)

                         Very satisfied 5
                         Satisfied 4
                         Neither satisfied
                           nor dissatisfied . 3
                         Dissatisfied 2
                         Very dissatisfied .. 1
                         Inappropriate 7
                         DK 8
                         NA 9   75. ____

76. People have different ideas about what they want out of a
    neighborhood organization. What is the most important
    thing that you would like?

    _____

    _____

    _____   76. ____

77. During the last year, have you talked to any of your neighbors
    about conditions in the neighborhood that bothered you?

                         Yes 1
                         No 0
                         DK .... 8 ⎫→ Skip to
                         NA .... 9 ⎭   Q79   77. ____

78. (If YES) Who was the first person that you contacted? Please
    give the first name or initials.

                    _____

                              SKIP TO Q81

79. If you were bothered by conditions in your neighborhood or by
    a neighborhood problem, would you normally talk to anyone in
    the neighborhood about it?

                         Yes 1
                         No 0
                         Inappropriate 7
                         DK .... 8 ⎫→ Skip to
                         NA .... 9 ⎭   Q96   79. ____

80. (If YES) Who would be the first person that you would
    contact (exclude spouse)? Please give first name or initials.

                    _____

81. Is ____ (name given in Q78 or Q80) one of the people we have
    previously discussed?
                         Yes 1
                         No 0
                         Inappropriate 7
                         DK .... 8 ⎫→ Skip to
                         NA .... 9 ⎭   Q83   81. ____

82. (If YES) Who?

    Person share common interests with (Q34) 4
    Important member of household (Q50) 3   FOR ANY ANSWER:
    #1 important person outside household (Q53) . 2 → Skip to
    #2 important person outside household (Q53) . 1   Q96
    Inappropriate 7   82. ____

83. (If NO) I would like to ask you a few questions about _____.

    (If not clear) Is _____ male or female?

    > Male 1
    > Female 2
    > Inappropriate 7   83. _____

84. Is _____ a relative, co-worker, neighbor or member of some
    organization? (CIRCLE ONLY ONE RESPONSE)

    > Grandfather .... 18 ⎤
    > Grandmother .... 17 |
    > Father .... 16 | **Skip to**
    > Mother .... 15 | ➤ Q94
    > Child .... 14 |
    > Brother/Sister .... 13 ⎦
    >
    > Relative 12
    > Co-worker 11
    > Neighbor 10
    > Member or neighborhood org ... 09
    > Member of church 08
    > Member of other org 07
    > Friend 06
    >
    > Government employee .... 05 ⎤
    > Minister, priest, rabbi ...... 04 |
    > Doctor .... 03 | **Skip to**
    > Counselor .... 02 | ➤ Q94
    > Other .... 01 |
    > Inappropriate .... 97 |
    > DK .... 98 |
    > NA .... 99 ⎦   84. _____

85. About how many years have you known _____? _____ (RECORD YEARS)   85. _____

86. About how old is _____? _____ (RECORD YEARS)   86. _____

87. Does _____ do the same kind of work (consider being a housewife
    work) as you do/did?

    > Yes 1
    > No 0
    > Inappropriate 7
    > DK 8
    > NA 9   87. _____

88. Is _____ presently:

    > Married 5
    > Widowed 4
    > Divorced 3
    > Separated 2
    > Never married 1
    > Inappropriate 7
    > DK 8
    > NA 9   88. _____

89. Does _____ have children?

    > Yes 1
    > No 0
    > Inappropriate 7
    > DK 8
    > NA 9   89. _____

90. What is _____'s ethnic (national) background?

    > _____   90. _____

91. What is _____'s religion?

    > _____   91. _____

92. Does _____ have more schooling than you do, about the same or
    less?

                              More 3
                              Same 2
                              Less 1
                              Inappropriate 7
                              DK 8
                              NA 9   92. _____

93. Is your contact with _____ generally

                              In person 4
                              By phone 3
                              Mixture of phone/
                                in person 2
                              By letter 1
                              Inappropriate 7
                              DK 8
                              NA 9   93. _____

94. How often do you usually get together with _____? (DO NOT READ
    RESPONSES)

                              About everyday 6
                              Once a week or more 5
                              Once a month or more 4
                              Several times a year 3
                              About once a year 2
                              Less than once a year ... 1
                              Inappropriate 7
                              DK 8
                              NA 9   94. _____

95. Where does _____ live? (DO NOT READ RESPONSES)

    In your neighborhood--say within a 10-
      minutes walk of your home 5
    In the city but outside your neighborhood ... 4
    Outside of the city but in the Pittsburgh
      metropolitan area (within 25 miles of
      your home) 3
    Outside of the metropolitan area but
      in Pennsylvania 2
    Outside of Pennsylvania 1
    Inappropriate 7
    DK 8
    NA 9   95. _____

Section IX: Network Density

IF ONLY ONE PERSON MENTIONED IN Q34, Q50, Q53 and Q83, SKIP TO Q97.

96. NOW I WOULD LIKE TO ASK YOU WHETHER THE PEOPLE WE HAVE DISCUSSED
    KNOW EACH OTHER.

    (INSTRUCTIONS: Take names given in Questions 34, 50, 53 and 83 and enter
    them below. List the names (up to 5) down the table and the first four
    (or one less than the number listed down) across the top in the same
    order. Ask whether Number 1 knows Number 2, whether Number 1 knows
    Number 3, and so on, going down column 1; then ask whether Number 2
    knows Number 3, whether Number 2 knows Number 4, and so on in column
    2, etc.)

	#1	#2	#3	#4	
	Do #1 and (2;3; 4;5) know each other?	Do #2 and (3;4; 5) know each other?	Do #3 and (4;5) know each other?	Do #4 and (5) know each other?	
#1					
#2	a. Yes......1 No.......0 Inapp....7 DK.......8 NA.......9				96a.____
#3	b. Yes......1 No.......0 Inapp....7 DK.......8 NA.......9	c. Yes......1 No.......0 Inapp....7 DK.......8 NA.......9			96b.____ 96c.____
#4	d. Yes......1 No.......0 Inapp....7 DK.......8 NA.......9	e. Yes......1 No.......0 Inapp....7 DK.......8 NA.......9	f. Yes......1 No.......0 Inapp....7 DK.......8 NA.......9		96d.____ 96e.____ 96f.____
#5	g. Yes......1 No.......0 Inapp....7 DK.......8 NA.......9	h. Yes......1 No.......0 Inapp....7 DK.......8 NA.......9	i. Yes......1 No.......0 Inapp....7 DK.......8 NA.......9	j Yes......1 No.......0 Inapp....7 DK.......8 NA.......9	96g.____ 96h.____ 96i.____ 96j.____

Section X: Other Organizations

97a. Some people belong to organizations such as church groups, PTAs, fraternal, union, little league and so on. Do you or members of your family belong to any of these organizations? (ONLY LIST THE THREE ORGANIZATIONS THAT THE RESPONDENT CONSIDERS THE MOST IMPORTANT.) (PROBE: Are there any others?)

IF NO ORGANIZATIONS ARE GIVEN, SKIP TO Q98

b. Where is the organization located? In or near your neighborhood, in the city but outside your neighborhood or outside the city?

c. Do any of your neighbors belong?

a. Organization Name:

#1	#2	#3	
_____	_____	_____	97a.____
_____	_____	_____	97b.____
_____	_____	_____	97c.____

b. <u>Location:</u>

	#1	#2	#3
In neighborhood	4	4	4
Near neighborhood	3	3	3
In city	2	2	2
Outside city	1	1	1
Inappropriate	7	7	7
DK	8	8	8
NA	9	9	9

(#1) 97d._____

(#2) 97e._____

(#3) 97f._____

c. <u>Neighbors Belong:</u>

	#1	#2	#3
Yes	1	1	1
No	0	0	0
Inappropriate	7	7	7
DK	8	8	8
NA	9	9	9

(#1) 97g._____

(#2) 97h._____

(#3) 97i._____

98. Have you done any volunteer work in the last year?

```
        Yes ................ 1
        No ................. 0
        DK ................. 8  ┐  Skip to
        NA ................. 9  ┘     Q101        98. _____
```

99. (If YES) Approximately how many hours per month do you spend doing this volunteer work?

_____ (RECORD ACTUAL #)   99. _____

100. Of the total amount of time that you have spent on volunteer activities, how much of that time has been related to your neighborhood? Was all of it, most, some or none?

```
        All ................ 4
        Most ............... 3
        Some ............... 2
        None ............... 1
        Inappropriate ...... 7
        DK ................. 8
        NA ................. 9                100. _____
```

Section XI: Work

101. Are you:

```
        Married ............ 6
        Divorced ........... 5 ┐
        Widowed ............ 4 │
        Separated .......... 3 │
        Single ............. 2 ├  Skip to
        Other .............. 1 │     Q105
        DK ................. 8 │
        NA ................. 9 ┘        101. _____
```

102. Is your spouse working full-time, part-time, unemployed, retired or what?

```
        Working full-time .. 6
        Working part-time .. 5
        Unemployed ......... 4
        Retired ............ 3
        Housewife .......... 2 ┐
        Other .............. 1 │
        Inappropriate ...... 7 ├  Skip to
        DK ................. 8 │     Q104
        NA ................. 9 ┘        102. _____
```

103. Where does (did) your spouse work? In or near the neighborhood, in other parts of the city, or in the suburbs?

           Neighborhood 4
           City 3
           Suburbs 2
           Outside Allegheny
             County 1
           Inappropriate 7
           DK 8
           NA 9   103. ____

104. How many years of school has your spouse completed? (Circle appropriate number)

           Elementary school .. 0 1 2 3 4 5 6
           Junior high school . 7 8 9
           High School 10 11 12
           College 13 14 15 16
           Post-College 17
           Vocational/technical 18
           G.E.D. 19
           Inappropriate 97
           DK 98
           NA 99   104. ____

105. Are you working full-time, part-time, unemployed, retired or what?

           Working full-time .. 6
           Working part-time .. 5
           Unemployed 4
           Retired 3
           Housewife 2
           Other 1   → Skip to
           DK 8   Q107
           NA 9   105. ____

106. Where do (did) you work? In or near the neighborhood, in other parts of the city or in the suburbs?

           Neighborhood 4
           City 3
           Suburbs 2
           Outside Allegheny
             County 1
           DK 8
           NA 9   106. ____

107. How many years of school have you completed?

           Elementary school .. 0 1 2 3 4 5 6
           Junior high school . 7 8 9
           High school 10 11 12
           College 13 14 15 16
           Post-college 17
           Vocational/technical 18
           G.E.D. 19
           DK 98
           NA 99   107. ____

108. In general, would you consider transportation to be a serious problem, a moderate problem, a minor problem or no problem at all in terms of getting to and from work for you (and/or your spouse)?

           Serious problem 4
           Moderate problem ... 3
           Minor problem 2
           No problem 1
           Inappropriate 7
           DK 8
           NA 9   108. ____

Section XII: Housing

109. Do you own or rent this home or apartment?

Own 2
Rent 1
DK 8
NA 9   109. ____

110. How would you rate this home/apartment in meeting the needs of
you and your family? Are you:

Very satisfied 5
Satisfied 4
Neither satisfied
nor dissatisfied . 3
Dissatisfied 2
Very dissatisfied .. 1
DK 8
NA 9   110. ____

RENTERS: SKIP TO Q112; HOMEOWNERS: ASK Q111

111. (For Homeowners) Have you made any major repairs or other im-
provements on your home during the past two or three years which
would have cost more than $500?

Yes 1
No 0
Inappropriate 7
DK 8
NA 9   111. ____

Section XIII: Public Services

112. I will mention some public services and would like you to tell
me if they are good, fair or poor in this neighborhood.

	Good	Fair	Poor	DK	NA	
a. Street repair maintenance	3	2	1	8	9	112a.____
b. Trash and garbage collection .	3	2	1	8	9	112b.____
c. Street cleaning	3	2	1	8	9	112c.____
d. Street lighting	3	2	1	8	9	112d.____
e. Police protection	3	2	1	8	9	112e.____
f. Fire protection	3	2	1	8	9	112f.____
g. Public transportation	3	2	1	8	9	112g.____
h. Traffic control (stop signs, stop lights)	3	2	1	8	9	112h.____
i. Animal control	3	2	1	8	9	112i.____

113. In general, how satisfied are you with the way the city provides
services in this neighborhood? Are you very satisfied, satisfied,
neither satisfied nor dissatisfied, dissatisfied or very dissatisfied?

Very satisfied 5
Satisfied 4
Neither satisfied
nor dissatisfied . 3
Dissatisfied 2
Very dissatisfied .. 1
DK 8
NA 9   113. ____

TURNING TO SCHOOLS FOR A MINUTE . . .

114. Do you have any children under 18?

```
                  Yes ................. 1
                  No .................. 0
                  DK .................. 8 ┐──► Skip to
                  NA .................. 9 ┘      Q118        114. _____
```

115. (If YES) (Does/Do) your (child/children) attend public, private or parochial school?

```
                  Private ............ 5
                  Parochial .......... 4
                  Public ............. 3
                  Public and private . 2
                  Public and parochial 1
                  Inappropriate ...... 7
                  DK ................. 8
                  NA ................. 9               115. _____
```

116. (Does/Do) your (child/children) attend school in or near your neighborhood? (AS LONG AS AT LEAST ONE CHILD ATTENDS SCHOOL IN THE NEIGHBORHOOD, SCORE IT "YES".)

```
                  Yes ................. 1
                  No .................. 0
                  Inappropriate ...... 7
                  DK ................. 8
                  NA ................. 9               116. _____
```

117. How would you rate the school? Are you very satisfied, satisfied, neither satisfied nor dissatisfied, dissatisfied or very dissatisfied?

```
                  Very satisfied ..... 5
                  Satisfied .......... 4
                  Neither satisfied
                    nor dissatisfied . 3
                  Dissatisfied ....... 2
                  Very dissatisfied .. 1
                  Inappropriate ...... 7
                  DK ................. 8
                  NA ................. 9               117. _____
```

Section XIV: Health

NOW WE HAVE A FEW QUESTIONS ABOUT YOUR OVERALL HEALTH . . .

118. How has your health been over the last year or so? Would you say you have been in poor health, fair health, good health or excellent health?

```
                  Poor health ........ 4
                  Fair health ........ 3
                  Good health ........ 2
                  Excellent health ... 1
                  DK ................. 8
                  NA ................. 9               118. _____
```

119. Now I would like to ask you about your life as a whole. In general are you very satisfied, satisfied, neither satisfied nor dissatisfied, dissatisfied or very dissatisfied with your life as a whole these days?

```
                  Very satisfied ..... 5
                  Satisfied .......... 4
                  Neither satisfied
                    nor dissatisfied . 3
                  Dissatisfied ....... 2
                  Very dissatisfied .. 1
                  DK ................. 8
                  NA ................. 9               119. _____
```

Section XV: Socioeconomic Data

WE ARE ABOUT FINISHED. I HAVE ONLY A FEW QUESTIONS LEFT TO ASK . . .

(INTERVIEWER: Where appropriate, RECORD ACTUAL NUMBER; DK=8, NA=9)

120. If there are any adults living in your household other than you
      and your spouse, would you please tell me their ages and relation-
      ship to you? (DO NOT READ RESPONSES)

   a. Number of other adults: _____ (RECORD ACTUAL #)   120a._____

   b. _____ (AGE)   c. Grandfather 09
                            Grandmother 08
                            Father 07
                            Mother 06
                            Brother 05
                            Sister 04
                            Child 03
                            Relative 02
                            Friend 01
                            Inappropriate 97   (AGE) 120b._____
                            DK 98
                            NA 99   (RELATIONSHIP) 120c._____

   d. _____ (AGE)   e. Grandfather 09
                            Grandmother 08
                            Father 07
                            Mother 06
                            Brother 05
                            Sister 04
                            Child 03
                            Relative 02
                            Friend 01
                            Inappropriate 97   (AGE) 120d._____
                            DK 98
                            NA 99   (RELATIONSHIP) 120e._____

   f. _____ (AGE)   g. Grandfather 09
                            Grandmother 08
                            Father 07
                            Mother 06
                            Brother 05
                            Sister 04
                            Child 03
                            Relative 02
                            Friend 01
                            Inappropriate 97   (AGE) 120f._____
                            DK 98
                            NA 99   (RELATIONSHIP) 120g._____

121. How many people are living in this household at present? _____   121. _____

122. How many are children under 18?   _____   122. _____

123. How old were you on your last birthday?   _____   123. _____

124. Do you own a car?

```
                    Yes ................ 1
                    No ................. 0
                    DK ................. 8
                    NA ................. 9              124. ____
```

125. Were you a registered voter during the last election?

```
                    Yes ................ 1
                    No ................. 0 ┐
                    DK ................. 8 ├──► Skip to
                    NA ................. 9 ┘      Q127       125. ____
```

126. Did you vote in the last election?

```
                    Yes ................ 1
                    No ................. 0
                    Inappropriate ...... 7
                    DK ................. 8
                    NA ................. 9              126. ____
```

127. How would you describe your ethnic (national) background?

```
    _____          127. ____
```

128. What is your religious preference?

```
                    Protestant ......... 01
                    Roman Catholic ..... 02
                    Orthodox Catholic .. 03
                    Jew ................ 04
                    Islam .............. 05
                    None ............... 06
                    Other .............. 07 (Specify: _____)
                    DK ................. 98
                    NA ................. 99              128. ____
```

129. We are interested in learning about the income levels in each
      of the neighborhoods in which we are interviewing; therefore, I
      would appreciate your telling me the range that includes your
      household's income before taxes last year. This should include
      income from all sources. (IF UNCERTAIN: What would be your
      best guess?)

      Is your income range below $10,000, between $10,000 and $25,000
      or above $25,000?

```
        Below $10,000
    WHICH CATEGORY OR        $3,000 or less ..... 01
    RANGE WOULD IT FALL      $3,001 to 7,000 .... 02
    INTO?  (READ CATEGORIES) $7,001 to 10,000 ... 03


        $10,000-$25,000      $10,001 to 13,000 .. 04
    WHICH CATEGORY OR        $13,001 to 16,000 .. 05
    RANGE WOULD IT FALL      $16,001 to 20,000 .. 06
    INTO?  (READ CATEGORIES) $20,001 to 25,000 .. 07


        Over $25,000         $25,001 to 30,000 .. 08
    WHICH CATEGORY OR        $30,001 to 40,000 .. 09
    RANGE WOULD IT FALL      $40,001 to 50,000 .. 10
    INTO?  (READ CATEGORIES) $50,001 and above .. 11

                    DK ................. 98
                    NA ................. 99              129. ____
```

130. Thank you for taking the time to help us with the survey. We have
talked about a lot of things. Is there anything that we missed
that could help to make your neighborhood a better place to live?

_____

_____

_____

_____

_____

_____

* * *

131. INTERVIEWER: Please note sex of respondent:

Male 1
Female 2   131. _____

Bibliography

Aberbach, Joel D., and Walker, Jack L. "The Attitudes of Blacks and Whites Toward City Services: Implications for Public Policy." In *Financing the Metroplis*, ed. John P. Crecine. Beverly Hills, Ca.: Sage, 1970.

Ahlbrandt, Roger S., Jr., and Brophy, Paul. *Neighborhood Revitalization: Theory and Practice.* Lexington, Ma.: Lexington Books, 1975.

Ahlbrandt, Roger S., Jr.; Charny, Margaret; and Cunningham, James V. "Citizen Perceptions of Their Neighborhoods." *Journal of Housing* (July 1977): 338–41.

Ahlbrandt, Roger S., Jr., and Cunningham, James V. *A New Public Policy for Neighborhood Preservation.* New York: Praeger, 1979.

Antonovsky, Aaron. *Health, Stress and Coping.* San Francisco: Jossey-Bass Publishers, 1979.

Attneave, Carolyn L. "Social Networks as the Unit of Intervention." In *Family Therapy: Theory and Practice,* ed. P. J. Guerin. New York: Gardner Press, 1976.

Barnes, James Allen. *Social Networks.* Reading, Ma.: Addison-Wesley, 1972.

————. "Networks and Political Process." In *Social Networks in Urban Situations,* ed. J. C. Mitchell. Manchester, England: University of Manchester Press, 1969.

Berkman, Lisa F., and Syme, S. Leonard. "Social Networks, Host Resistance and Mortality: A Nine-Year Follow-Up Study of Alameda County Residents." *American Journal of Epidemiology* 109(2) (1979): 186–204.

Biegel, David E., and Naparstek, Arthur J., ed. *Community Support Systems and Mental Health.* New York: Springer Publishing, 1982.

Birch, David L.; Brown, Eric S.; Coleman, Richard P.; DaLomba, Delores W.; Parsons, Williams L.; Sharpe, Linda C.; and Weber, Sheryll A. *A Behavioral Model of Neighborhood Change.* Boston: Joint Center for Urban Studies of the Massachusetts Institute of Technology and Harvard University, 1977.

Birch, David L., et al. *The Community Analysis Model.* Boston: Joint Center for Urban Studies of the Massachusetts Institute of Technology and Harvard University, 1977.

Blau, Peter M. "Structural Effects." *American Sociological Review* 25 (April 1960): 178–93.

Bott, Elizabeth. *Family and Social Network: Norms and External Relationships in Ordinary Urban Families.* London: Tavistock Publications, 2nd ed. rev., 1971.

Bradburn, Norman M. *The Structure of Psychological Well-Being.* Chicago: Aldine, 1969.

Bradbury, Katherine. "Housing Supply Policies: An Examination of Partial Equilibrium Impacts in a Metropolitan Area." Discussion Paper # 418–77. Madison, Wi.: University of Wisconsin, Institute for Research on Poverty, 1977.

Campbell, Angus; Converse, Philip E.; and Rodgers, Willard L. *The Quality of American Life: Perceptions, Evaluations and Satisfaction.* New York: Russell Sage Foundation, 1976.

Caplan, Gerald. *Support Systems and Community Mental Health: Lectures on Concept Development.* New York: Behavioral Publications, 1974.

Caplan, Gerald, and Killilea, Marie. *Support Systems and Mutual Help.* New York: Grune and Stratton, 1976.

Caplan, R. D., et al. *Adhering to Medical Regimes: Pilot Experiments in Patient Education and Social Support.* Ann Arbor: Institute for Social Research, 1976.

Cassel, John. "The Contribution of the Social Environment Host Resistance." *American Journal of Epidemiology* 102(2) (1976): 107–23.

Cobb, Sidney. "Social Support and Health Through the Life Cycle." Paper presented at the Annual Meeting of the American Association for the Advancement of Science, 1978.

————. "Social Support as a Moderator of Life Stress." *Psychosomatic Medicine* 38(5) (1976): 300–14.

Collins, Alice H., and Pancoast, Diane L. *Natural Helping Networks.* Washington, D.C.: National Association of Social Workers, 1976.

Cooperman, D., and Hagoel, L. "Community in Southdale." *CURA Reporter* 10 (June 1980): 12–15.

Craven, Paul, and Wellman, Barry. "The Network City." *Sociological Inquiry* 43 (1973): 58–88.

Davis, James A.; Spaeth, Joe L.; and Huson, Carolyn. "A Technique for Analyzing the Effects of Group Composition." *American Sociological Review* 26 (April 1961): 215–25.

Dean, Alfred, and Lin, Nan. "The Stress-Buffering Role of Social Support: Problems and Prospects for Systematic Investigation." *Journal of Nervous and Mental Disease* 165(6) (1977): 403–17.

DeLeeuw, Frank. "The Distribution of Housing Services: A Mathematical Model." Working Paper No. 208–1. Washington, D.C.: Urban Institute, November 1971.

DeLeeuw, Frank, and Struyk, Raymond J. *The Web of Urban Housing.* Washington, D.C.: The Urban Institute, 1975.

Downs, Anthony. *Neighborhoods, Urban Development and Public Policies.* Washington, D.C.: Brookings Institution, 1981.

Eaton, William W. "Life Events, Social Supports and Psychiatric Symptoms: A Reanalysis of the New Haven Data." *Journal of Health and Social Behavior* 19 (1978): 230–34.

Emerson, Richard. "Power–Dependence Relations." *American Sociological Review* 27 (February 1962): 31–41.

Feagin, Joe. "Community Disorganization." *Sociological Inquiry* 43 (Winter 1973): 123–46.

Fischer, Claude S.; Jackson, Robert M.; Stueve, C. Ann; Gerson, Kathleen; and McCallister-Jones, Lynne; with Baldassare, Mark. *Networks and Places: Social Relations in the Urban Setting.* New York: Free Press, 1977.

Fowler, Floyd. *Citizen Attitudes Toward Local Government, Services and Taxes.* Cambridge, Ma.: Ballinger, 1974.

Fried, Marc, and Gleicher, Peggy. "Some Sources of Residential Satisfaction in an Urban Setting." In *Neighborhood, City and Metropolis,* eds. Robert Gutman and David Popenoe. New York: Random House, 1970.

Gans, Herbert J. *The Levittowners.* New York: Vintage, 1967.

————. *The Urban Villagers.* New York: Free Press, 1962.

Gerson, Kathleen; Stueve, C. Ann; and Fischer, Claude S. "Attachment to Place." In *Networks and Places,* Claude S. Fischer, et al. New York: Free Press, 1977.

Goering, John M. "Neighborhood Tipping and Racial Transitions: A Review of Social Science Evidence." *Journal of the American Institute of Planners* 44 (January 1978): 68–78.

Goetze, Rolf. *Building Neighborhood Confidence.* Cambridge, Ma.: Ballinger, 1976.

Gore, Susan. "The Effects of Social Support in Moderating the Health Consequences of Unemployment." *Journal of Health and Social Behavior* 19 (1978): 157–65.

Granovetter, Mark. "The Strength of Weak Ties." *American Journal of Sociology* 78 (May 1973): 1360–80.

Greer, Scott. *The Emerging City.* New York: Free Press, 1962.

Grigsby, William C., and Rosenberg, Louis. *Urban Housing Policy.* New York: APS Publications, 1975.

Groves, Robert M., and Kahn, Robert L. *Surveys by Telephone: A National Comparison with Personal Interviews.* New York: Academic Press, 1979.

Gurin, Gerald; Veroff, Joseph; and Feld, Sheila. *Americans View Their Mental Health.* New York: Basic Books, 1960.

Homans, George C. *Social Behavior.* New York: Harcourt Brace Jovanovich, 2nd ed. 1974.

House, James S. *Work Stress and Social Support*. Reading, Ma.: Addison-Wesley, 1980.

Hunter, Albert. "The Loss of Community." *American Sociological Review* 40 (October 1975): 537–52.

————. *Symbolic Communities*. Chicago: University of Chicago Press, 1974.

Ingram, Gregory K.; Kain, John F.; and Ginn, Royce J. *Detroit Prototype of the NBER Urban Simulation Model*. New York: National Bureau of Economic Research, 1972.

Janowitz, Morris. *The Community Press in an Urban Setting*. Chicago: University of Chicago Press, 1967.

Kagan, A. R., and Levi, L. "Health and Environment—Psychosocial Stimuli: A Review." *Social Science and Medicine* 8 (1974): 225–41.

Kain, John F., and Quigley, John M. *Housing Markets and Racial Discrimination: A Microeconomic Analysis*. New York: National Bureau of Economic Research, 1975.

Kaplan, Bertram H.; Cassel, John C.; and Gore, Susan. "Social Support and Health." *Medical Care* 25 (1977): 47–58.

Kasarda, John D., and Janowitz, Morris. "Community Attachment in Mass Society." *American Sociological Review* 39 (June 1974): 328–39.

Laumann, Edward O. *Bonds of Pluralism*. New York: Wiley, 1973.

Leven, Charles L.; Little, James T.; Nourse, Hugh O.; and Read, R. B. *Neighborhood Change: Lessons in the Dynamics of Urban Decay*. New York: Praeger, 1976.

Liebow, Elliott. *Tally's Corner*. Boston: Little, Brown, 1967.

Lin, Nan; Ensel, Walter M.; Simeone, Ronald S.; and Kuo, Wen. "Social Support, Stressful Life Events and Illness: A Model and an Empirical Test." *Journal of Health and Social Behavior* 29 (1979): 108–19.

Litwak, Eugene, and Szelenyi, Ivan. "Primary Group Structures and Their Functions: Kin, Neighbors and Friends." *American Sociological Review* 34 (August 1969): 465–81.

Lovrich, Nicholas P., Jr., and Taylor, G. Thomas, Jr. "Neighborhood Evaluation of Local Government Services." *Urban Affairs Quarterly* 12 (December 1976): 197–222.

Michelson, William. *Environmental Choice, Human Behavior and Residential Satisfaction*. New York: Oxford University Press, 1977.

Mitchell, J. Clyde. "The Concept and Use of Social Networks." In *Social Networks in Urban Situations*, ed. J. Clyde Mitchell. Manchester: University of Manchester Press, 1969.

Muth, Richard F. *Cities and Housing*. Chicago: University of Chicago Press, 1969.

Nisbet, Robert A. *The Quest for Community*. New York: Oxford University Press, 1969.

Nuckolls, Katherine B.; Cassel, John; and Kaplan, Bertram H. "Psychosocial Assets, Life Crisis and the Prognosis of Pregnancy." *American Journal of Epidemiology* 95 (1972): 431–41.

President's Commission on Mental Health. *Task Panel Reports Submitted to the President's Commission on Mental Health, vol. 2.* Washington, D.C.: U.S. Government Printing Office, 1978.

Public Affairs Counseling. *The Dynamics of Neighborhood Change.* Washington, D.C.: U.S. Government Printing Office, 1975.

Raphael, Beverley. "Preventive Intervention with the Recently Bereaved." *Archives of General Psychiatry* 34 (1977): 1,450–54.

Real Estate Research Corporation. *Analysis of Data on Neighborhood Preservation Program Areas.* Chicago: Real Estate Research Corp., 1976.

Schuman, Howard, and Gruenberg, Barry. "Dissatisfaction with City Services: Is Race an Important Factor?" In *People and Politics in Urban Society,* ed. Harlan Hahn. Beverly Hills, Ca.: Russell Sage, 1971.

Selye, Hans. "Forty Years of Stress Research: Principal Remaining Problems and Misconceptions." *CMA Journal* 115 (1976): 53–6.

Sewell, William H., and Armer, Michael J. "Neighborhood Context and College Plans." *American Sociological Review* 31 (April 1966): 159–68.

Silverman, Phyllis R. "The Widow to Widow Program: An Experiment in Preventive Intervention." *Mental Hygiene* 53 (1969): 333–37.

Simmel, Georg. *Conflict and the Web of Group Affiliations.* Trans. by K. H. Wolff and R. H. Bendix. New York: Free Press, 1922, 1955.

Stack, Carol B. *All Our Kin.* New York: Harper and Row, 1974.

Stegman, Michael. *Housing Investment in the Inner City: The Dynamics of Decline.* Cambridge, Ma.: The MIT Press, 1972.

Stein, Maurice R. *The Eclipse of Community.* New York: Harper and Row, 1960.

Sternlieb, George. *The Urban Housing Dilemma.* New York: New York City Housing Development Administration, 1972.

Sternlieb, George, and Burchell, R. W. *Residential Abandonment: The Tenement Landlord Revisited.* New Brunswick, N.J.: Rutgers University Press, 1973.

Straszheim, Mahlon R. *An Econometric Analysis of the Urban Housing Market.* New York: National Bureau of Economic Research, 1975.

Struyk, Raymond J.; Marshall, Sue A.; and Ozanne, Larry J. *Housing Policies for the Urban Poor.* Washington, D.C.: The Urban Institute, 1978.

Suttles, Gerald D. *The Social Construction of Communities.* Chicago: University of Chicago Press, 1972.

———. *The Social Order of the Slum.* Chicago: University of Chicago Press, 1968.

Thibaut, J., and Kelly, H. H. *The Social Psychology of Groups.* New York: Wiley, 1959.

Timms, Duncan W. G. *The Urban Mosaic: Towards a Theory of Residential Differentiation.* Cambridge, England: Cambridge University Press, 1971.

Walker, Gerald. "Social Networks and Territory in a Commuter Village, Bond Head, Ontario." *Canadian Geographer* 21 (Winter 1977): 329–50.

Warren, Donald I. *Helping Networks: How People Cope with Problems in the Urban Community.* Notre Dame, Ind.: The University of Notre Dame Press, 1981.

————. *Black Neighborhoods: An Assessment of Community Power.* Ann Arbor: University of Michigan Press, 1975.

————. "Explorations in Neighborhood Differentiation." *Sociological Quarterly* 19 (Spring 1973): 310–31.

Warren, Rachelle B., and Warren, Donald I. *The Neighborhood Organizer's Handbook.* Notre Dame, Ind.: The University of Notre Dame Press, 1977.

Webber, Melvin M. "Order in Diversity: Community Without Propinquity." In *Neighborhood, City and Metropolis,* eds. Robert Gutman and David Popenoe. New York: Random House, 1970.

Wellman, Barry. "The Community Question: The Intimate Networks of East Yonkers." *American Journal of Sociology* 84 (March 1979): 1,201–31.

Wellman, Barry; Craven, Paul; Whitaker, Marilyn; Dutoit, Sheila; and Stevens, Harvey. "The Uses of Community." Research Paper No. 47. Toronto: Center for Urban and Community Studies, University of Toronto, 1971.

Wellman, Barry. "Networks, Neighborhoods and Communities: Approaches to the Study of the Community Question." *Urban Affairs Quarterly* 14 (March 1979): 363–90.

Whyte, William Foote. *Street Corner Society.* Enlarged ed. Chicago: University of Chicago Press, 1955.

Yin, Robert K. *Conserving America's Neighborhoods.* New York: Plenum Press, 1982.

Index